2011 NOTE
Keep - OUT OF PRINT
HARD TO FIND.

By ALFRED McCLUNG LEE

The Daily Newspaper in America: The Evolution of a Social Instrument
Race Riot (with Norman D. Humphrey)
Principles of Sociology (editor, co-author)
Readings in Sociology (editor, co-author)
How to Understand Propaganda
Public Opinion and Propaganda (co-editor, co-author)
Fraternities Without Brotherhood
La Sociologia delle Comunicazioni (UNESCO lectures)
Che Cos'è la Propaganda (Fulbright lectures)
Multivalent Man

By ELIZABETH BRIANT LEE

Personnel Aspects of Social Work in Pittsburgh
Eminent Women: A Cultural Study
Mental Health and Mental Disorder: A Sociological Approach (co-editor)

By ALFRED McCLUNG LEE and ELIZABETH BRIANT LEE

Social Problems in America
Marriage and the Family

The Fine Art of Propaganda

*Prepared for the Institute
for Propaganda Analysis*

by

ALFRED McCLUNG LEE

and

ELIZABETH BRIANT LEE

With a new introductory essay

OCTAGON BOOKS

A DIVISION OF FARRAR, STRAUS AND GIROUX

New York 1972

Reprinted 1972

by special arrangement with the authors

OCTAGON BOOKS

A DIVISION OF FARRAR, STRAUS & GIROUX, INC.

19 Union Square West

New York, N. Y. 10003

LIBRARY OF CONGRESS CATALOG CARD NUMBER: 79-159206

ISBN 0-374-94860-7

Printed in U.S.A. by
NOBLE OFFSET PRINTERS, INC.
New York, N.Y. 10003

TO

those writers, editors, and other specialists in communication who do what they can to fulfil the promise of the First Amendment to the Constitution of the United States of America

Contents

Introduction to the Octagon Edition:

The Imperative Art: Propaganda Analysis

THE TWENTIETH is the century of vast power in mass communications. During it, as media have multiplied and expanded, specialists in publicity methods have developed propaganda into a "fine art" of appalling effectiveness. Thus, the citizen who does not want to be a mere pawn, who hopes to have intellectual dignity and integrity, in other words who wishes to think for himself, can well look upon propaganda analysis as the "imperative art." Since before the days of Socrates, it has been the necessary defense against mass-manipulators as well as against individual confidence men.

Why did "propaganda analysis" spread quickly through the programs of adult study groups and the curricula of high schools and colleges following 1937? Why did it then just as quickly, only four years later, change into something else?

The San Francisco *News's* editor[1] asserted in 1937 that propaganda analysis "is one more weapon for democracy in the ceaseless battle against obfuscation and special interest." The Hartford *Courant's* editor[2] added: "The less gullible the public becomes through understanding, the less danger there is of action, political, economic or social, being based on emotion." He called propaganda analysis "commendable and worthy of encouragement."

These editors were talking about the non-profit Institute for Propaganda Analysis. It stimulated this wave of interest in propaganda analysis. That organization had highly prestigious officers and board members drawn from leading universities and colleges. It was born on a flood of hope and controversy in 1937. The late Boston merchant, Edward A. Filene, sparked the venture with a $10,000 grant from his Good Will Fund, and that fund made some additional grants to the Institute after Filene's death. Columbia University Professor Clyde R. Miller became its first executive as a switch from his previous labors as Teachers College's successful publicist. By 1939, *Newsweek*[3] hailed propaganda analysis as "one of the newest and fastest growing ideas in American education" and credited the Institute with its development and dissemination.

Propaganda analysis "caught on so readily," in the view of the Institute's staff,[4] "because it provided a badly needed perspective for current affairs. The age of miracles through which America passed up to 1929 produced a large amount of gullibility. In place of the healthy skepticism for which the Yankee was noted, and which was enshrined in such sayings as 'I'm from Missouri; show me,' Americans had come to believe in a slow but sure progress toward the millenium. Journalistic muckraking was all but forgotten. H. L. Mencken poked bubbles for a few years in the *American Mercury*, and 'debunking' biographies appeared frequently, but the success stories of the *American Magazine* put the other literature in the shade. The public relations expert appeared on the scene and the captains of industry, the bankers, politicians, college officials and even prize fighters became philosophers given to salty sayings and filled with beneficent concern for the public weal. The seamy side of life was lost to view; anyone who mentioned it was a misanthrope. The dream would not last. The depression brought the cold awakening. By 1937 people were ready and waiting for a corrective, and propaganda analysis provided the needed scientific lens.

"Seen through this medium, the moves came to be understood as not merely the exasperating results of tasteless fumbling but rather the channel through which selected idea stereotypes are paraded as the pattern of American life. The newspapers, commonly thought of as enterprises in which an editor makes decisions with Olympian detachment, were shown to be creatures of their business, social and popular relationships, influenced by the biases of the business community from which the advertising comes, the biases of the publisher and his social circle and those of the readers, whose patronage is needed to interest the advertisers. The radio, likewise, was seen to be influenced by the biases of the advertisers, the government officials involved in regulation, and the listening public.

"Similarly the leading propagandists of the day ceased to appear as mere individuals. Some proved to be the spokesmen for significant social points of view. When the ideas of Father Coughlin were viewed in the light of the seven propaganda devices it became evident that he was not the harmless crackpot many had thought; he was playing with fascism, drawing many of his state-

ments word for word from German propaganda literature. A striking example of pro-democratic propaganda
recently cited by the Institute [in *Propaganda Analysis,*
the bulletin dated August 26, 1941] was that of Negro
groups, who are reminding their white fellow-citizens
that Hitler's ideas of racial superiority are widely prac-
tised, even though generally condemned, over here.

"Thus the analysis of any major propaganda gives an
insight into the social forces which the propaganda
represents. So propaganda analysis—the search behind
the propagandist's words to see what he is trying to
accomplish—becomes an approach to the study of current social issues. It is a method as old as Socrates, as
has often been pointed out, but so many ideas have
come to be taken for granted that the study of them
has all the novelty of exploration."

And so the Institute launched a wave of publicity and
of formal education for propaganda analysis. In the
Bronx's Evander Childs High School, instruction even
took the form of a musical morality play, "Snow White
and the Seven Propaganda Devices." The Gullible
Public as Snow White was perplexed about the Neu-
trality Act. The seven dwarfs of propaganda gave her a
rough time until she was rescued by her Prince Charm-
ing, none other than Critical Thinking. The theme
chorus of the dwarfs was:

> "Oh, we are the seven devices,
> We turn up in time of crisis;
> We play upon your feeling,
> We set your brain a-reeling.
> We are seven active contrabanders,
> We are seven clever propaganders."[5]

In addition to the direct use of its materials in high school and college classes with an estimated enrollment of 100,000 students and in uncounted adult groups, the Institute granted 231 requests in four years for the reprinting of its materials in textbooks, general works, encyclopaedias, articles, lectures, and sermons. These were the extensive, word-for-word reproductions; short quotations and paraphrases did not require such permissions. "The Institute had correspondence with 2500 teachers regarding the use of its materials; it had correspondence with 1200 adult study groups of all kinds—branches of the American Association of University Women, Leagues of Women Voters, trade unions, peace groups, religious groups, Y.M.C.A., Y.W.C.A., Y.M.H.A., settlement houses and W.P.A. groups."[6]

The publications of the Institute consisted of fifty regular numbers of *Propaganda Analysis: A Bulletin to Help the Intelligent Citizen Detect and Analyze Propaganda,* a series of *Decide-for-Yourself Packets* each containing 15 to 25 pieces of original propaganda material related to the subject of a bulletin's report, bound annual volumes of *Propaganda Analysis,* and such special volume-length studies as the *Group Leader's Guide to Propaganda Analysis* and *The Fine Art of Propaganda.* In addition, the Institute cooperated in the preparation of many pamphlets, booklets, and books issued by such other organizations as "America's Town Meeting of the Air," the Williamstown Institute of Human Relations, the *Survey Graphic,* and the *Christian Science Monitor.*

And then, shortly after Pearl Harbor Day, the Institute issued a bulletin entitled "We Say Au Revoir." Its reasons for "dying" were as notable and as symptomatic as were its enthusiastic welcome and acceptance only a little more than four years earlier. Here they are, as set forth in the concluding number of its bulletin on January 9, 1942[7]:

"The publication of dispassionate analyses of all kinds of propaganda, 'good' and 'bad,' is easily misunderstood during a war emergency, and more important, the analyses could be misused for undesirable purposes by persons opposing the government's efforts. On the other hand, for the Institute, as an Institute, to propagandize or even to appear to do so would cast doubt on its integrity as a scientific body. If it were to continue it would have to analyze all propaganda—of this country and of Britain and Russia as well as of Germany, Italy and Japan.

"The Board of Directors considered this problem at its meeting on February 27, 1941. It decided then that if the United States became engaged in actual hostilities a meeting should be held at once to consider the Institute's course. President Roosevelt's announcement that the United States had entered the 'shooting stage' of the War came on October 27 [1941]. By that time there was pressure from both interventionists and anti-interventionists to make partisan analyses of the other fellow's propaganda. Also, good friends and former supporters became convinced that since we could not be partisan, their own effort to aid democracy in the crisis should be made elsewhere; that long-time programs like the Institute's could wait. Students of public opinion were bound to see the possibilities of misunderstanding and danger to the Institute's program inherent in such a situation. The Board of the Institute met on October 29, examined the various courses open to it, and decided upon suspension of the Bulletin.

"The suspension occurs at a time when the most valuable part of the Institute's work is at the height of its influence. This part of the work is the demonstration of methods by which people can analyze propaganda for themselves. It remains available and unimpaired by controversy or hysteria. The publications showing the method are in public libraries, schools and colleges all over the country, where they can be consulted and studied. Since war situations bring forth much vicious propaganda—although much good propaganda as well—the Institute's reports thus far should find increasing use. The intolerance that usually accompanies and immediately follows war periods has already appeared. It can and must be combatted if we are to avoid here the Nazism and fascism we are opposing. It can be combatted by the methods of propaganda analysis popularized by the Institute. . . .

"Analysis is one antidote for the propaganda that is intended to turn people against minorities; analysis and a refusal to be stampeded by *name-calling* until the justice of the name has been established. More important are national policies that avoid frustrations; policies that do not give rise to false hopes; policies that make sacrifices worth while; above all policies that demonstrate through actual works the ability of democracy to serve its people's needs.

"Propaganda, as has been pointed out, must fit the facts of experience or be discredited. This is true of both 'good' and 'bad' propaganda. With the understanding of the roots of propaganda, which the Institute has sought to reveal, it is possible to defeat false kinds. The human ground can be made more resistant to the seeds of intolerance. The Institute for Propaganda Analysis hopes its work has contributed to that end."

The Institute as an entity thus did not survive the continuing militarized atmosphere of World War II, the subsequent wars in Korea and Indo-China, and the so-called "interwar" periods. Its publications and the many works inspired by them nevertheless continue to make their stimulating contributions to education and to public discussion not only in this country but throughout the world. The managerial-technician bias has gained increasing strength in "liberal arts" high schools and colleges, and this tends to propagate and strengthen courses for propaganda "producers" in public relations, publicity, mass communications, public opinion surveying, and related topics. But the traditional—that is, the "consumer's"—emphasis in liberal arts continues and with it education in propaganda analysis. This emphasis appears in courses in logic, sociology, social psychology, political science, consumer economics, social group work, and public speaking. Many standard texts for all such courses continue to quote from and to cite Institute materials and to apply them in fresh contexts. Thus many still agree with the late great social historian and publicist, Harry Elmer Barnes,[8] when he called the Institute's work "the most important single educational enterprise in the United States today so far as preparation for the democratic way of life is concerned."

REFERENCES

1. Editorial page, San Francisco *News,* October 7, 1937.
2. Editorial page, Hartford *Courant,* November 8, 1937.
3. "Analysis of Propaganda: Institute Teaches How to Bare Influences on Public Opinion," *Newsweek,* April 3, 1939. See also "Anti-Propaganda Institute Reports 4,000 Subscribers," *Editor & Publisher,* February 26, 1938.
4. "We Say Au Revoir," *Propaganda Analysis,* vol. 4, no. 13 (January 9, 1942), pp. 3–4. See also Curtis D. MacDougall, *Understanding Public Opinion* (New York: Macmillan Co., 1952), chap. 4.
5. *Newsweek,* April 3, 1939.
6. "We Say Au Revoir," *op. cit.,* p. 3.
7. *Ibid.,* pp. 1, 6.
8. *Ibid.,* p. 2. See also A. McC. Lee, *How to Understand Propaganda* (New York: Rinehart & Co., 1952), pp. 27–28.

THE FINE ART
OF PROPAGANDA

I. Cracker Barrels and Radios

AROUND the storied cracker barrel at the crossroads grocery store, the local intellectuals, politicians, and men-about-the-township have gathered since colonial days to dispute local issues, to weigh the destinies of rulers and nations, to decide the means for solving international crises, and to condemn and praise efforts to change the traditional moral code. The grocer, with a watchful eye on his crackers, has had a ready jest with which to keep his guests from becoming too acrid.

Around the cracker barrel, a spirit of friendly good sportsmanship has been the treasured tradition. The following remarks, repeated many times over, reflect this sturdy democratic attitude:

"Yeah, you said the same thing when they were goin' to build the new bridge over Breakneck Creek."

"How d'yuh know?"

"Who told you?"

"Well, who's he? What right has he got to tell us what we should do and not do?"

"You better bring that book over here and show me where you got that stuff. It don't sound right."

"My cousin told me how it worked over at Milltown, and I'm against it. I don't care what those down-state politicians have to say for it."

This way of reaching conclusions by give-and-take around the local cracker barrel or the stove in the railroad station or the fireplace in the Commercial Hotel or the counter in the corner tobacco shop has pervaded our national life. It has been carried directly into the New England town meetings and the councilmanic hearings in our smaller governmental units throughout the country. In print, it has taken the form of letters to editors. And the graduates of the cracker barrel circles have gone on to places in our state and national legislative halls and administrative offices, on the whole taking with them the cracker-barrel philosophy of fair play.

But now our country has become much larger and, at the same time, much more closely knit together than ever before. In addition to discussions in the grocery stores, at lodge meetings, on the lawn in front of church after services, etc., we find ourselves becoming parts of powerful pressure groups that have leaders who speak in behalf of large segments of our population. These pressure groups are not all the same. They do not all have policies worked out in the open through a give-and-take discussion by their memberships. Some have policies formulated by outstanding individuals and offered to us to accept or not as we see fit. How such leaders reach their conclusions, from what facts and for what purposes, is not always clear.

Pressure groups represent a necessary addition in large-scale democracy to the cracker barrel and the town meeting. They furnish the means for making the wishes of large sections of our population known during election battles and afterwards during legislative and administrative contests. They include many admirable organizations: our churches, our trade and professional associations and unions, our political parties, our patriotic societies, etc.

But we need to be forever on our guard for the other kind of pressure groups. These groups have men at their helms who are not controlled by policies determined through democratic processes, who do not represent a known membership, and who seek to lead those who believe in them over paths other than those they announce. To such men, little matters except the power they obtain through arousing the emotions of those who do not understand the uses of rabble-rousing propaganda.

These subtle propagandists, who parade their devotion to American principles while attempting to undermine them, represent factors in our society that sometimes militate against the best uses of discussion. As Walter Lippmann has written, "The private citizen today has come to feel rather like a deaf spectator in the back row." Too often, he adds, we see public affairs "managed, if they are managed at all, at distant centers, from behind scenes, by unnamed powers." What are these powers? Whose invisible hands pull the strings that make certain things happen? Why do we "think" and act and vote in prescribed ways when certain strings are pulled and then find ourselves—too late—to have been deluded?

In this modern world, the spokesmen for undemocratically organized and operated pressure groups have the same incalculably powerful instruments of communication at their hands as have the leaders of the democratic pressure groups. Many of us still gather around cracker barrels and cigar counters and in beauty shops, but the radio, the newspaper, and the periodical have become means for a clever man to reach a national and even international audience. To an amazing extent these mediums have replaced the face-to-face discussion of issues in the twentieth century.

And what are the characteristics of these new means for disseminating ideas? How do they differ from the cracker barrel and the old-time newspaper and periodical?

Let us talk first about similarities. Then the differences will stand out more clearly.

As our newspapers and periodicals have grown in size to become huge mass-production enterprises, their editors have—with a few notable exceptions—attempted to keep their news and feature materials fairly representative of the differing interests of their readers. Regardless of editorial policies, newspapers in particular have felt compelled to report the chief campaign speeches of those representing at least our two major political parties. Church pages carry Catholic, Jewish, and Protestant information without favor. Although labor union news has been slighted and frequently misunderstood, improvements are observable in this department. And readers may still take their pens or typewriters in hand, tell their editor what they think of his views, and have a reasonable chance of seeing their literary effort in print. In short, despite shortcomings that have been so well described of late, the American press tries to maintain a spirit of give-and-take in its pages, to give the reader the facts and statements of opinion by the chief spokesmen for opposing pressure groups.

The radio had little significance as a mass-communication device until well into the 1920's. It groped, as it so rapidly grew, for policies that would fit in with the American scheme of things. As it became more and more conscious of popular interest in news, views, speeches, dramas, and church services, the well-tested theories of the cracker-barrel circle—as they had been modified to work under mass-production conditions by daily newspapers—were taken over and again modified.

Letters to editors became sidewalk interviews with passing citizens. In place of news articles reviewing the speeches of opposing leaders, the radio was able to bring the actual speeches into our homes. During any political campaign, we can dial in talks by representatives of at least the two major parties and usually an occasional discussion by the minority party candidates. Over any week-end, we can take our choice among services or programs of a wide variety of Protestant, Jewish, and Roman Catholic congregations.

Here, too, therefore, despite the shortcomings of this instrument so well described of late, the American broadcasting systems and individual stations try to maintain a spirit of give-and-take in their programs, to give their listeners the facts and statements of opinion by the chief spokesmen for opposing pressure groups.

But speeches, especially as they are delivered over the radio, inject a new and startling factor into our political, economic, and social processes. Except for such admirable programs as "The Town Meeting of the Air," those who listen to a speaking program are left wholly at the mercy of the orator's word-magic. The spell cannot be broken by hecklers. At the end of a talk, the speaker is not confronted with the obligation to answer questions and meet objections from the floor. Shout as you will at your radio, the only recourse you have is to turn off the power, far from a satisfying alternative to getting your questions answered. If only we had two-way radio communication, especially during a speech broadcast! Many a speaker would then hear, thundering back to him across the air waves, shouts of:

"Let's hear *all* of that quotation!"

"You say that that source is reliable, but let's have convincing proof."

"Yeah, but down here in Crossroads Center, we tried out that idea on the school board, and look what happened."

The situation is well illustrated by speeches during the Presidential campaign of 1936. The chief speechmakers were Franklin D. Roosevelt, Alfred M. Landon, and John D. M. Hamilton. There were, in addition, a scattered group of minority representatives and independents who included Norman Thomas, Earl Browder, William Lemke, and the Rev. Charles E. Coughlin. All of these men paid glowing tributes to democracy. Even though they placed divergent interpretations on what democracy means and offered different solutions for current problems, the three majority representatives and Thomas and Browder spoke as recognized leaders of regularly organized pressure groups. They held known positions in known political parties. Their talks smacked of the cracker barrel. Roosevelt, Landon, and Hamilton had known political careers behind them. Thomas and Browder, the Socialist and Communist candidates, had both played prominent roles for many years in the minority parties that had nominated them for the Presidency. To those who did not know Thomas and Browder, their political party labels were adequate identifications. But such orators as Lemke and Father Coughlin were different. Lemke was chiefly known as Father Coughlin's candidate. And who was Father Coughlin?

Father Coughlin was a priest who had discovered the power of his thoughts and his voice when they were spread broadcast by radio. In 1928, as he asserted in a radio "lecture" on March 6th ten years later, "I was happy to cast my lot with those whom capitalism and so-called democracy were exploiting in the name of sound economics and of sound government." He had then transformed a Sunday afternoon talk for children into weekly "educational talks on economics and politics." As the processes of self-discovery and audience-discovery progressed, his language had become more and more intemperate and emotional. His political and economic theories, always nebulous, gradually unfolded and exhibited the quasi-socialistic characteristics so useful to Hitler in his rise to power.

"In politics," Father Coughlin likes to say, "I am neither Republican, Democrat, nor Socialist. I glory in the fact that I am a simple Catholic priest endeavoring to inject Christianity into the fabric of an economic system woven upon the loom of greed by the cunning fingers of those who manipulate the shuttles of human lives for their own selfish purposes." Let's see how he did this in the 1936 Presidential campaign:

Father Coughlin had spoken wildly in 1932-34 of "Roosevelt *or* Ruin." Or, as he explained this crusade on March 6, 1938, "I became a public sponsor of the New Deal because it pledged to drive the money changers and their servants from the temple." By 1934, however, he "began to suffer the pangs of disillusionment." He had "discovered" that the "fundamental economic error which had characterized the administration of Hoover, of Coolidge and their predecessors in office, was accepted by the New Deal." Old Deal and New Deal, he now came to believe, differed only "accidentally"; "one was the left wing and the other the right wing of the same bird of prey." He began in 1934 and continued throughout the 1936 campaign, therefore, to declaim about "Roosevelt *and* Ruin." He called the President of the United States a "liar" and a "scab President" and asserted that with Roosevelt in 1933-37 and with Landon in 1937-41 "there would be nothing left for America but bloody revolution." The only alternative, he insisted, was his own candidate, William Lemke.

Father Coughlin's significance in the 1936 campaign and later is not that he obtained many votes for his Presidential candidate. He did not. On August 15, 1936, he stated at Cincinnati that, "if I cannot swing at least 9,000,000 votes to Mr. Lemke, I will quit broadcasting educational talks on economics and politics." The official record reveals that Lemke received 891,858 votes. Within a week after that election, Coughlin asserted:

I am hereby withdrawing from all radio activity in the best interests of all the people. I am doing this without attempting to offer one alibi, thereby proving that my promise is better than my bond.

Father Coughlin's significance lies in the manner in which he has utilized his gifts to inject into the "thinking" of certain groups of uncritical Americans such undemocratic factors—factors that are not tolerated around our cracker barrels—as repeated falsehoods, bitter name-calling, race hatred, and proposals of "bullets instead of ballots," techniques so effectively used by European dictators.

Even though few Americans voted for Lemke in 1936, Father Coughlin's propaganda methods interest us because they are typical of the utterances of a surprisingly large group of anti-democratic speakers in the United States. Among these Father Coughlin stands out as one of the more noisy. According to *Propaganda Analysis* for January 1, 1939, "Today in the United States there are some 800 organizations that could be called pro-fascist or pro-Nazi. Some flaunt the word 'Fascist' in their name, or use the swastika as their insignia. Others—the great majority—talk blithely of democracy, or 'Constitutional Democracy,' but work hand in glove with the outspokenly fascist groups and distribute their literature. All sing the same tune—

words and music by Adolf Hitler, orchestration by Dr. Paul Joseph Goebbels. . . . It can be sung with variations, but always the refrain is 'Jew!' and 'Communist!' "

Since the 1936 election and Father Coughlin's voluntary retirement and then return to the radio, he has become more openly fascist in his methods and his pronouncements. On Sunday, March 13, 1938, he revealed his purposes so far as to advocate the reorganization of the United States into a "Corporate State" very similar to the set-up in Fascist Italy. Just as Hitler obtained socialist backing in Germany through using socialistic terminology and calling his party National Socialist, so Father Coughlin is attempting to align lovers of democracy with his objectives through advocating a "democratic Corporate State free from the domination of capitalism and partyism; free from bigotry and racial hatreds." He insists that his proposals are "not imported from communistic Russia, from socialistic Germany, or from fascistic Italy" and are not "to be identified with the so-called totalitarian state in which all citizens exist for the state." As illustrations in succeeding chapters of this book bring out, however, he cries down "bigotry" and then advocates a single national religion, recognized by the state; he lectures against "racial hatreds" and then devotes hours of radio time to the cultivation of anti-Jewish prejudices; he calls for "class co-operation instead of class hatred" and then demands direct Federal dictatorship of employer-employee relations and Congressional representation along trade-association and trade-union lines, with an undemocratic weighting of power on the side of trade associations and other property interests; and he condemns "radicalism" and then attempts to undermine popular faith in the Federal Constitution, in business leadership, in financial management, in labor unions, and in our chosen governmental representatives.

It is little wonder that such an admittedly anti-democratic organization as Fritz Kuhn's German-American Bund has become enthusiastic about Father Coughlin's "educational talks on economics and politics." According to Miss Dorothy Thompson, columnist for the New York *Herald Tribune*, writing on February 22, 1939, "An alliance has been formed in this country between the followers of Father Coughlin and the followers of Fritz Kuhn to abolish the American democracy as we have known it since the days of Lincoln." She mentions "a Coughlin meeting in a New York armory at which Bund literature and tickets . . . were distributed." At a Bund meeting in Madison Square Garden, too, Bund speakers made "numerous references to Father Coughlin's leadership." The audience cheered his name.

As *Propaganda Analysis* for January 1, 1939, noted, "The American people had yawned in his face when he cried 'Roosevelt and Ruin,'" and, therefore, Father Coughlin needed a more potent formula. And such a formula was apparently ready-made, waiting to be tried: "To America's would-be dictators, *Mein Kampf* is Horatio Alger, Jr., stream-lined. Mr. Alger's hero didn't smoke or swear or drink, he saved his money, loved his mother, and rose from rags to riches, Q.E.D. The hero of *Mein Kampf* shrieked 'Jew!' and 'Communist!' and he, too, rose from rags to riches—from poverty-stricken housepainter to Chancellor of Germany."

The utterances of the "would-be Hitlers" of our 800 fascist and near-fascist organizations would never get far around one of our traditional cracker barrels, and they are not becoming as yet a serious threat to American democracy in our new world of mass discussion. But these anti-democratic spokesmen have made themselves sufficiently noisy to warrant an analysis of the methods they typically use. Above all, an impartial scientific analysis of the techniques of one furnishes a pattern for getting to the bottom of the propagandas of others as they are brought to our attention. We can thus create in our own minds a keener type of thinking that will in part make up for the decline in opportunities for cracker barrel discussions.

In the following pages, we discuss the general and personal—the social and psychological—characteristics of propaganda and then take up the methods of propagandists. Illustrations of these "tricks of the trade" are drawn from the radio addresses of Father Coughlin.

II. Our Bewildering Maze of Propaganda

THE WORLD is beset today by a confusion of conflicting propagandas, a Babel of voices in many tongues shouting charges, counter-charges, assertions, and contradictions that assail us continually.

These propagandas are spread broadcast by spokesmen for political parties, labor unions, business associations, farm organizations, patriotic societies, churches, schools, and other agencies. And they are repeated in conversation by millions of individuals.

If American citizens are to have a clear understanding of conditions and what to do about them, they must be able to recognize propaganda, to analyze it, and to appraise it. They must be able to discover whether it is propaganda in line with their own interests and the interests of our civilization or whether it is propaganda that may distort our views and threaten to undermine our civilization.

Propaganda more than ever is an instrument of aggression, a new means for rendering a country defenseless in the face of an invading army. While it has been used in a halting way for centuries, within the past few years we have seen it prepare the way for Hitler to seize the Saar, Austria, the Sudetenland and Czechoslovakia. It is called a new instrument of aggression because development has given it an effectiveness never before experienced in the history of the world.

Never before has there been so much propaganda. Never before have there been so many propagandas of such great importance to the lives of all of us. And never before have there been such powerfully implemented propagandas. The modern news-gathering systems of the newspapers and the gigantic radio broadcasting facilities of the world have made the chief differences, but refinements in propagandist methods have kept pace.

As generally understood, *propaganda is opinion expressed for the purpose of influencing actions of individuals or groups*. More formally, the Institute for Propaganda Analysis has defined propaganda as "expression of opinion or action by individuals or groups deliberately designed to influence opinions or actions of other individuals or groups with reference to predetermined ends."

Propaganda thus differs fundamentally from scientific analysis. The propagandist tries to "put something across," good or bad. The scientist does not try to put anything across; he devotes his life to the discovery of new facts and principles. The propagandist seldom wants careful scrutiny and criticism; his object is to bring about a specific action. The scientist, on the other hand, is always prepared for and wants the most careful scrutiny and criticism of his facts and ideas. Science flourishes on criticism. Dangerous propaganda crumbles before it.

Because the action sought by a propagandist may be beneficial or harmful to millions of people, it is necessary to focus upon his activities the same searchlight of scientific scrutiny that the scientist invites. This requires a considerable effort. We all have a tendency to make a virtue of defending opinions or propagandas that apparently fit in with our own opinions and of opposing as vigorously any others. But socially desirable views and proposals will not suffer from examination, and the opposite type will be detected and revealed for what it is.

Propagandas which concern us most are those which alter public opinion on matters of large social consequence —often to the detriment of large sections and even the majority of the people. Such propagandas, for example, are involved in these issues:

Hitler, Mussolini, and many dignitaries of the Roman Catholic Church *are right or wrong* in supporting Franco.

Chamberlain and Daladier *saved or undermined further* the peace of Europe through their efforts at appeasement—at "buying off" the dictators of Germany and Italy; and

The C.I.O., the A. F. of L., and the National Association of Manufacturers *are or are not* obstructing efforts to merge the C.I.O. and the A. F. of L.

Any effort to analyze the propagandas involved in the public discussion of such cases as these confronts us first with the seven ABC's of Propaganda Analysis. We must have the feel of these seven ABC's before we can fully appreciate the uses made by propagandists of the seven Propaganda Devices, the "Tricks of the Trade" described in the next chapter. Our seven ABC's are:

*A*SCERTAIN the conflict element in the propaganda you are analyzing. All propaganda contains a conflict element in some form or other—either as cause, or as effect, or as both cause and effect.

*B*EHOLD your own reaction to this conflict element. It is always necessary to know and to take into consideration our own opinions with regard to a conflict situation about which we feel strongly, on which we are prone to take sides. This information permits us to become more objective in our analysis.

*C*ONCERN yourself with *today's* propagandas associated with *today's* conflicts. These are the ones that affect directly our income, business, working conditions, health, education, and religious, political, and social responsibilities. It is all too easy to analyze some old example of propaganda, now having little relation to vital issues.

*D*OUBT that your opinions are "your very own." They usually aren't. Our opinions, even with respect to today's propagandas, have been largely determined for us by inheritance and environment. We are born white or black, Catholic, Protestant, Jewish, or "pagan"; rich or poor; in the North or East, South or West; on a farm or in a city. Our beliefs and actions mirror the conditioning influences of home and neighborhood, church and school, vocation and political party, friends and associates. We resemble others with similar inheritance and environment and are bound to them by ties of common experience. We tend to respond favorably to their opinions and propagandas because they are "our kind of people." We tend to distrust the opinions of those who differ from us in inheritance and environment. Only drastic changes in our life conditions, with new and different experiences, associations, and influences, can offset or cancel out the effect of inheritance and long years of environment.

*E*VALUATE, therefore, with the greatest care, *your own propagandas*. We must learn clearly *why* we act and believe as we do with respect to various conflicts and issues—political, economic, social, and religious. Do we believe and act as we do because our fathers were strong Republicans or lifelong Democrats; because our fathers were members of labor unions or were employers who fought labor unions; because we are Methodists, Seventh Day Adventists, Catholics, or Jews? This is very important.

*F*IND THE FACTS before you come to any conclusion. There is usually plenty of time to form a conclusion and believe in it later on. Once we learn how to recognize propaganda, we can most effectively deal with it *by suspending our judgment until we have time to learn the facts and the logic or trickery involved in the propaganda in question.* We must ask:

Who is this propagandist?

How is he trying to influence our thoughts and actions?

For what purpose does he use the common propaganda devices?

Do we like his purposes?

How does he use words and symbols?

What are the exact meanings of his words and symbols?

What does the propagandist try to make these words and symbols appear to mean?

What are the basic interests of this propagandist?

Do his interests coincide with the interests of most citizens, of our society as we see it?

GUARD always, finally, against *omnibus words*. They are the words that make us the easy dupes of propagandists. Omnibus or carryall words are words that are extraordinarily difficult to define. They carry all sorts of meanings to the various sorts of men. Therefore, the best test for the truth or falsity of propaganda lies in specific and concrete definitions of the words and symbols used by the propagandist. Moreover, sharp definition is the best antidote against words and symbols that carry a high charge of emotion.

Our seven Propaganda Devices make the application of these seven ABC's of Propaganda Analysis somewhat easier. Before describing these devices, however, let us discuss the nature of propaganda further by answering some pertinent questions regarding it:

When does a propaganda conform to democratic principles? It conforms when it tends to preserve and extend democracy; it is antagonistic when it undermines or destroys democracy.

"What is truly vicious," observed the New York *Times* in an editorial on September 1, 1937, "is not propaganda but a monopoly of it." Any propaganda or act that tends to reduce our freedom in discussing important issues—that tends to promote a monopoly of propaganda—is anti-democratic.

How broadly should we define democracy? Democracy has the four following aspects, set forth or definitely implied in the Constitution and the Federal statutes:

1. *Political*—Freedom to discuss fully and effectively and to vote on public issues.

2. *Economic*—Freedom to work and to participate in organizations and discussions to promote better working standards and higher living conditions.

3. *Social*—Freedom from oppression based on theories of superiority or inferiority of group, class, or race.

4. *Religious*—Freedom of worship, with separation of church and state.

With all such general freedoms and the specific freedoms implied by them are associated definite responsibilities. Thus, with freedom of the press goes the responsibility for accuracy in news and honesty and representativeness in editorials. These responsibilities were summed up once and for all by Jesus Christ in His Sermon on the Mount as follows:

Therefore all things whatsoever ye would that men should do to you, do ye even so to them: for this is the law and the prophets.

In short, democracy is the one political, economic, and social philosophy which permits the free expression and development of the individual in a culture.

Why are we sometimes misled by propaganda antagonistic to democracy? Few people have had the opportunity to learn how to detect and analyze propaganda. Most books on propaganda are for the benefit of the propagandist or the academic specialist rather than of the public.

They are frequently in such technical terms that they may be understood only by persons familiar with the nomenclature of psychology and sociology. Furthermore, most of these treatises deal with the propagandas of the past, not of today. It is *today's propagandas, flowing from today's conflicts*, which interest and concern us most.

Is there any popular recognition of the need to analyze facts, alleged facts, opinions, propagandas? Yes. It is implied in the public forum movement; in the privately printed letters for business men prepared by such as the Kiplinger Washington Agency, and Harland Allen; in the New York *Herald Tribune* Annual Forum on Current Problems; in various college conferences on economics, politics, and world issues; in reports and programs of the Foreign Policy Association; in the privately circulated reports of the Consumers' Union; in the addresses and discussions of educators, clergymen, and editors at the Williamstown Institute of Human Relations; and in various radio programs, including the "University of Chicago Round Table," "The Town Meeting of the Air," and the "People's Platform."

"Propaganda," said an editorial in the Springfield (Mass.) *Republican*, September 3, 1937, "is good as well as bad. 'We are surrounded by clouds of propaganda.' . . . It is up to each of us to precipitate from those clouds the true and the false, the near-true and the near-false, identifying and giving to each classification its correct label."

How nearly right are our answers? The Institute lays no claim to infallibility. It tries to be scientific, objective, and accurate. When it makes mistakes, it acknowledges them. It asks the readers of this book as well as the subscribers for its regular bulletin, *Propaganda Analysis*, to check its work further and also to co-operate with it by supplying documented evidence on the sources of propaganda and on censorship or distortion of essential news in press, radio, and newsreels. Chiefly the Institute seeks to acquaint its subscribers and other readers of its materials with methods whereby they may become proficient in making their own analyses.

III. The Tricks of the Trade

SOME of the devices now so subtly and effectively used by good and bad propagandists are as old as language. All have been used in one form or another by all of us in our daily dealings with each other.

Propagandists have seized upon these methods we ordinarily use to convince each other, have analyzed and refined them, and have experimented with them until these homely devices of folk origin have been developed into tremendously powerful weapons for the swaying of popular opinions and actions.

We have all emphasized our disapproval of a person, group, or thing by calling it a bad name. We have all tried to reverse this process in the case of something for which we have had admiration by labeling it with a "virtue word" or "glittering generality." And thus, we have all used two of the propaganda devices.

In order to avoid technical language, in order to make our findings more generally useful, the popular terms for these propagandistic devices have been retained here. Considerable experience with them by scientific analysts, business men, teachers, and college and high school students indicates that they have the two necessary qualifications for our purpose: *They are workable. Anyone can use them.*

The chief devices used then in popular argument and by professional propagandists—together with our symbols for them—are:

1. *Name Calling,* symbolized by the ancient sign of condemnation used by the Vestal Virgins in the Roman Coliseum, a thumb turned down . . . .

2. *Glittering Generality,* symbolized by a glittering gem that may or may not have its apparent value

3. *Transfer,* symbolized by a mask such as was worn by ancient Greek and Roman actors . . . .

4. *Testimonial,* symbolized by a seal and ribbons, the "stamp of authority" . . . .

5. *Plain Folks,* symbolized by that traditional analogue for an old friend, an old shoe . . . .

6. *Card Stacking,* symbolized by an ace of spades, a card traditionally used to signify treachery . . . . . .

7. *Band Wagon,* symbolized by a bandmaster's hat and baton, such as were once used on old-fashioned band wagons . . . .

To explain fully the uses to which these simple-sounding devices are being put by professional propagandists requires more than a brief definition. It is necessary, rather, to read through a selection of actual examples such as are given in the eight following chapters of this book. In the next seven, each of the seven devices is illustrated in turn. In the final chapter, a complete speech of Father Coughlin is taken and analyzed in considerable detail in terms of all these devices and of the facts.

But a brief definition can give the gist of each. It is therefore possible and certainly desirable to get the following thumbnail descriptions of each before us:

Name Calling—giving an idea a bad label—is used to make us reject and condemn the idea without examining the evidence.

Glittering Generality—associating something with a "virtue word"—is used to make us accept and approve the thing without examining the evidence.

🏵 *Transfer* carries the authority, sanction, and prestige of something respected and revered over to something else in order to make the latter acceptable; or it carries authority, sanction, and disapproval to cause us to reject and disapprove something the propagandist would have us reject and disapprove.

🜲 *Testimonial* consists in having some respected or hated person say that a given idea or program or product or person is good or bad.

👃 *Plain Folks* is the method by which a speaker attempts to convince his audience that he and his ideas are good because they are "of the people," the "plain folks."

[•] *Card Stacking* involves the selection and use of facts or falsehoods, illustrations or distractions, and logical or illogical statements in order to give the best or the worst possible case for an idea, program, person, or product.

🜚 *Band Wagon* has as its theme, "Everybody—at least all of *us*—is doing it"; with it, the propagandist attempts to convince us that all members of a group to which we belong are accepting his program and that we *must therefore* follow our crowd and "jump on the band wagon."

Once we know these devices well enough to spot examples of their use, we have taken a great and long step towards freeing our minds from control by propagandists. It is not the only step necessary, but it is certainly the most important.

Once we know that a speaker or writer is using one of these propaganda devices in an attempt to convince us of an idea, we can separate the device from the idea and see what the idea amounts to on its own merits. The idea may be good or bad when judged in the light of available evidence and in terms of our own experience and interests. But a knowledge of these seven devices permits us to investigate the idea. It keeps us from having our thought processes blocked by a trick. It keeps us from being fooled.

In testing each statement of a propagandist, then, we merely have to ask ourselves: *When stripped of tricks, what is he trying to sell us? Is it something we want?*

The Following Chapters. Illustrations of the "Tricks of the Trade" are drawn in the following chapters from many of the "educational talks on politics and economics" delivered by the Rev. Charles E. Coughlin on Sunday afternoons in 1938 and early in 1939, especially on November 6, 1938, to January 1, 1939. The latter were especially recorded for the purpose and were then checked with the printed version distributed by Father Coughlin from his Shrine of the Little Flower at Royal Oak, Michigan, in a booklet entitled *Am I an Anti-Semite? 9 Addresses on Various "Isms" Answering the Question.*

Name Calling—Giving an idea a bad label—
is used to make us reject and condemn the
idea without examining the evidence.

IV. Name Calling

BAD NAMES have played a tremendously powerful role
in the history of the world and in our own individual development. They have ruined reputations, stirred men and
women to outstanding accomplishments, sent others to
prison cells, and made men mad enough to enter battle
and slaughter their fellowmen. They have been and are
applied to other people, groups, gangs, tribes, colleges,
political parties, neighborhoods, states, sections of the country, nations, and races.

The world has resounded with cries of "Heretic,"
"Hun," "Red," "Yankee," "Reb," "Democrat," "Republican," "Revolutionary," "Nazi," etc., and their equivalents
in all languages. Our personal lives have echoed with such
words as "sissy," "moron," "bully," "tramp," "wayward,"
"unscientific," "unprogressive," "inhuman," "grasping,"
"easy-going," and "backward."

Individuals and groups can be found who bear any one
of these labels proudly. Other individuals and groups can
just as easily be found who regard any one of these labels
as the worst epithet to shout at an enemy.

Practically all primitive tribes call themselves by names
that mean "the people" or "the real people." All out-
siders they call "foreigners," "earth-eaters," "cannibals,"

"ill-speakers," or some other term they regard as dispreputable. The Welsh, for example, called themselves the Cymry, but our present term for the Welsh derives from an Anglo-Saxon word meaning "foreigners" or "jabberers."

One of the most treacherous things about Name Calling is that bad names, like Glittering Generalities, are *omnibus words*. They are words that mean different things and have different emotional overtones for different people. When we spot an example of Name Calling, we must ask ourselves these questions:

What does the name mean?

Does the idea in question—the proposal of the propagandist —have a legitimate connection with the real meaning of the name?

Is an idea that serves my best interests and the best interests of society, as I see them, being dismissed through giving it a name I don't like?

In other words, leaving the name out of consideration, what are the merits of the idea itself?

We must constantly remind ourselves of the danger of omnibus-word reactions. Such reactions, rather than detailed appraisals of a philosophy and its ideals, are what we commonly encounter.

Father Coughlin's Name Calling. As the following chapters illustrate, Father Coughlin depends chiefly upon three devices with which to prove his points: Transfer (Chapter VI), Testimonial (Chapter VII), and Card Stacking (Chapter IX). But the four other "Tricks of the Trade," especially Name Calling and Glittering Generality (Chapter V), bolster up his "sales talk" at innumerable points.

In illustrating Father Coughlin's uses of Name Calling,

it is of course necessary to use quotations and summaries of parts of his speeches that involve applications of other propaganda devices as well. This is not regarded as a handicap but rather as a decided advantage, for it shows how several devices are in most cases used together. Symbols will not be used here, however, to spot illustrations of tricks other than Name Calling; that would be confusing at this stage. A similar procedure is followed in the six succeeding chapters. Then, in Chapter XI, all seven symbols are used together.

In his recent speeches, Father Coughlin's chief bad names are "world-wide subversive activities," "imported radical," "atheistic Jew," "Communist Jew," "international Jew," "internationalism," "Nazism," "Communism," "the economic system," "money changer," and "international banker." His use of all of these may well be illustrated with one of his examples "taken from next week's issue of *Social Justice*," his "news" magazine, and with an "important principle" he announced on November 20, 1938.

The first two of the Coughlin bad names listed appear in these two paragraphs from his lecture of January 22, 1939:

Few of you know that Prague, the capital of Czechoslovakia, until recently was the headquarters of world-wide subversive activities ⟨image⟩, and fewer of you possess the information that these headquarters in part have been removed to Dublin, Ireland, this past month and a half. The current stories, therefore, appearing in our newspapers blaming the Irish people for the English bombings are only half truths. Our news weekly points out that this propaganda proposes to liquidate the good esteem which Christians over the world entertain towards Neville Chamberlain, the Prime Minister of England, through the agency of the imported radicals ℞ from Czechoslovakia into Ireland whom they have concentrated at Dublin. They are the ones, and not the Irish, who are responsible for the bombings for which the Irish Republicans are blamed.

Those of us who happened to hear these comments *and then suspended judgment* on Father Coughlin's allegations until more facts appeared soon learned from another Irish-American source the following, which is quoted from a news story in the New York *World-Telegram* of March 1, 1939:

The Clan na Gael, secret Irish patriotic society, and the Irish Republican Army Veterans, Inc., have united here "to support the recent bombings in Britain," it was disclosed today.

About 350 representatives of Irish organizations met at the Clan and veterans' headquarters, 537 W. 125th St., Sunday night and formed the United Irish Republicans, which they hope to be the biggest movement in this country for Irish unity since 1921.

Michael J. Quill, City Councilman and president of the Transport Workers Union, was one of the speakers and, according to the new organization, predicted Irish-American support of "the warfare in England." . . .

A member of the Clan na Gael . . . said local clans over the country had protested against a radio talk in which Father Coughlin blamed the bombings on Prague Communists who had fled to Dublin after Czechoslovakia recapitulated to Germany.

They got no acknowledgment or correction, so now the clans are "keeping tabs" on Father Coughlin's Sunday radio talks, said this member.

In short, Father Coughlin had either no evidence or distorted evidence upon which he based his Name Calling attack on the Czechoslovaks and his unsought "defense" of the Irish Republican Army.

The other Coughlin bad names in the foregoing list are linked together in what Father Coughlin has chosen to enunciate as an "important principle." This principle is, according to his speech of November 20th, as follows:

Thus, if Nazism, a persecutor of Jew and Catholic and Protestant—if Nazism is a defense mechanism against Communism, be assured that Communism, another persecutor, was a defense mechanism against the greed of the money changers ⚑, who persecuted ⚑, then pilloried ⚑ the teeming populations of Europe. Permit me to repeat that important principle. If Nazism is now memorable for its injustice ⚑ and its persecution ⚑, so was Communism. And so was the economic system ⚑ which made slaves ⚑ of millions in the midst of plenty; the system ⚑ which generated Communism.

This principle, quite similar to that of the official Nazi propagandists, may be stripped down to somewhat simpler English with the aid of other passages in the November 20th address and presented in this form:

The bad Jews ⚑ and bad Gentiles ⚑, as greedy money changers ⚑ and international bankers ⚑, used the materialistic economic system ⚑ to persecute ⚑ and pillory ⚑ the teeming populations of Europe. This persecution led to Communism, a "defense mechanism" against the bad Jews ⚑ and bad Gentiles ⚑. Communism, inspired by atheistic Jews ⚑ and atheistic Gentiles ⚑, then persecuted ⚑ the Catholics and Protestants *but not* the Jews, good or bad. Because of its internationalism ⚑, Communism became such a threat ⚑ to German civilization that the Nazis were able to introduce National Socialism as a "defense mechanism" against Communism. The Nazis then persecuted the Jews, Catholics, and Protestants.

Father Coughlin has never stated this "important principle" in such lucid English. If he had, its inconsistencies, its fundamental absurdity, might have been apparent to some of his followers. Let us pass over the theory as a whole for the present, however, and analyze each of his questionable "bad names" scientifically. Let us suspend our judgment upon his Name Calling until we have examined the meaning—as accepted by reputable authorities—of his labels.

This theory has been interpreted in the United States as being primarily an attack upon the Jews. As the Rev. W. C. Kernan, Rector of Trinity Episcopal Church, Bayonne, New Jersey, stated in a radio address during his WEVD "Free Speech Forum" on February 16, 1939:

It will be noted that in the statement of Father Coughlin quoted above he places Gentiles with Jews as the agents responsible for Communism. It may be further noted that throughout his speeches are interlarded with references to atheistic Jews and Gentiles, the purpose being to make us think that the speaker is harmlessly impartial.

But, as he proceeds, the Gentile agents who are responsible for Communism gradually cease to be of importance. The weight of his argument is gradually but certainly thrown against the Jews. Thus, he goes on to say that "it is the belief of the German government, be it well or ill founded, that Jews were responsible for the economic and social ills suffered by the Fatherland since the signing of the Treaty of Versailles." Our attention is drawn here only to Jews. Nothing is said about the German dislike for the Treaty of Versailles itself, which was drawn up by Gentiles.

Let us look then at the factual basis for Father Coughlin's insistence upon linking "atheistic," "international," and "Communist" with "Jew." And, since the implication here —substantiated by repeated direct statements in his November 20th and other lectures—is that he regards the Jew as a member of a special Jewish race, not just a believer in certain religious principles, let us first approach these Coughlin bad names by answering two questions: What is a race? What is a Jew?

What is a race? A direct answer to this question has been summarized from scientific anthropological literature —but in popular terms—by Dr. Ellsworth Faris of the University of Chicago. It is as follows:

> If we inquire as to the number of races, we learn that some anthropologists make three races, others five, and so on through a varying number up to nineteen; and the point is that however many or few there may prove to be, they are all made, that is, constructed.
>
> The members of the human species vary through a continuous series, and the division into races has always something in it of the arbitrary. It is easy to distinguish the Chinese, the Swedes, and the Bantus from one another, but if we try to divide the whole of mankind into races there remain unsolved problems and peoples that are not fitted into any division. This does not mean that there are no races, but it does mean that men who talk glibly about race often do not realize the difficulty of their subject.

This is the consensus of opinion among the leading anthropologists of the United States and the world. In other words, almost none of us *even looks like* pure Nordics, Negroes, Semites, Alpines, Mongolians, or whatnot. A "pure Nordic" is about as common as an albino, even in Germany.

What is a Jew? Dr. M. R. Davie of Yale University, in his *World Immigration*, answers this question as follows:

> The Jews have no racial type but a bond of racial sympathy. That which makes the Jews a peculiar people is not the little Semitic blood they may possess, but their cultural traits and

experience. There are no differences between Jews and Christians which can justly be attributed to racial causes, and which depend solely on hereditary transmission, unaffected by the environment. Culturally, there is nothing unusual in the fact that an isolated community should evolve peculiar characteristics. The chief culture trait of the Jews is their religion which they all have in common. Associated with it is their common religious language, Hebrew, and the careful training of their children in the Law. As a result of their religion they have all suffered persecution. They have also through the force of special circumstances specialized in certain occupations, chiefly commerce, the clothing industry, and money-lending. Through occupation, the need of protection, and legal restrictions they have also become extraordinarily urbanized. The Gentiles by centuries of oppression of the Jew have fostered in him precisely those points of difference which tend to become contentions.

Adolf Hitler, the great tub-thumper for Nordic and "Aryan" superiority, is a fairly typical member of the race to which most Jews belong, the Alpine.

In short, a Jew is a German, Frenchman, Chinese, American, Russian, Abyssinian, or some other national who is a member and exhibits the cultural characteristics of one of the Jewish religious sects. Racially, they are quite mixed, have little Semitic blood, and are in fact frequently Alpine. Like other loose aggregates of people, they fall into rather sharp divisions among themselves. From a political standpoint, they have fought on each side of many wars in Europe and America and have contributed leaders and voters to all our political parties. Another type of division is described by Elizabeth Stern in her book, *I Am a Woman and a Jew*. She points out that "the aristocratic Spanish Jew scorns the plebeian German Jew; the prosperous German Jew looks with hauteur on the Polish and

Russian Jew. The Russians and the Poles, on their part, return with good measure the blighting disapproval of the German Jew, and accept with proper spirit the patronage of the Spanish Jew."

In other words, Jews are stupid and brilliant, poor and rich, members of all sorts of political parties, citizens of every nation except such countries as Germany where they have been deprived of this status. All that they have in common is that their religions are sects preserving or branching out of the ancient faith of Israel, the religious, ethical, and social teachings of the Old Testament, and that this fact and their wanderings color their other customs and behavior patterns.

With these facts before us, we can now assess Father Coughlin's use of the term, "atheistic Jew." From the foregoing, it is obvious that this is a slur against the Jews, an effort to link Orthodox, Reformed, and other Jews to the activities of those who may once have believed in the teachings of a Jewish sect. It is as unfair to accept this relationship as it is to believe the scurrilous tales once circulated by so-called "unfrocked priests" and "fugitive nuns." It is in a class with speaking of "atheistic Catholics" or "atheistic Methodists."

With these important questions answered by experts, we are now also in a position to analyze the bad names, "Communist Jew" and "international Jew." These terms also need to be assessed scientifically in the light of authentic facts. In doing so, the following questions are answered:

Can a person be both a Communist and a Jew?
What are the attitudes of leading Jews and Jewish organizations on political and economic issues?

Is "internationalism" fairly used as a bad name, synonymous with Communism?

The answers given below to these questions indicate whether or not Father Coughlin is using these terms in a fair and descriptive manner. They reveal whether or not Father Coughlin speaks of "Communist Jews" and "international Jews" in a way that disparages all Jews. Let us examine the evidence:

Can a person be both a Communist and a Jew? In answer to this question, one finds substantial agreement among those chiefly involved, the Jews and Communists. They would answer: *No.* A member of the Communist party in the Soviet Union is required to renounce all former religious beliefs as "capitalistic opiates," whether Protestant, Roman Catholic, Jewish, Russian Orthodox, or other. The *Manifesto of the Communist Party*, written by Karl Marx and Friedrich Engels and originally published in 1847, as well as other statements by Marx, Lenin, and Stalin, makes it abundantly clear that *Communism opposes all established religions but does not oppose any person or group because of racial heritage.* The reflection of this position in the policies of the Communist Party of the United States has been stated as follows by Earl Browder, its Secretary:

We stand without any restrictions for education that will root out beliefs in the supernatural, that will remove the religious prejudices which stand in the way of organizing the masses for Socialism, that will withdraw the special privileges of religious institutions. But as far as religious workers go, the Party does not insist that they abandon their beliefs before they join the Party. Our test for such people is whether they represent and fight for the aspirations of the masses. If they do, we welcome them into our Party, and we exercise no coercion against their religious beliefs within our movement. We subject their religious beliefs to careful and systematic criticism, and we expect that they will not be able to withstand this educational process.

This quotation from Browder's handbook, *What is Communism?*, alters but slightly the traditional Marxian fight against the "religious opiate."

The two points mentioned—the opposition of Communism to religion and the refusal of Communism to recognize race differences—are both essential to an understanding of the distortions of impression with which Coughlin has slurred the Jews in the present connection. They will both be referred to again elsewhere.

The reasons for Jewish opposition to Communism have been well summarized in a scholarly booklet by Father Joseph N. Moody, Ph.D., entitled, *Why are Jews Persecuted?* (1938). Father Moody is Professor of European History at Cathedral College, St. Louis, and his work bears the imprimatur of Archbishop John J. Glennon of St. Louis and is published by The Queen's Work, Inc. He points out that the Jews "have suffered more than the rest of the (Russian) population from Soviet tyranny," that the "Jewish religion has been proscribed with the same fervor as was the Christian and the Mohammedan," and that the "Hebrew language is strictly forbidden." He mentions the confiscation of synagogues, the exiling of prominent rabbis, and the placing of thirty-five per cent of the Jewish population in the "category of *déclassés*" or "class enemies who have no legal or economic rights" in contrast with "only five per cent of the non-Jewish population who are thus branded as pariahs."

Professor Hugo Valentin, a noted historian on the faculty of Upsala University, Sweden, gives a similar summary of the status of the Jews under Russian Communism in his scholarly work, *Antisemitism, Historically and Critically Examined.* He reports that a "boundless misery swept over the Jewish as over the non-Jewish bourgeoisie." Since "the Jewish population consisted to a far greater extent than the Christian of middle-class folk—two-fifths of the Jews of Russia lived by private trade, one-third by handicrafts," he has found that "the putting in force of Communism meant a greater catastrophe for the Jews than for any other section of the Russian people."

From a popular as well as from an anthropological and sociological standpoint, this sectarian analysis of the Coughlin term, "Communist Jew," requires modification. Popularly and scientifically, and even in certain Jewish circles, a Jew remains a Jew even after he has given up membership in and even belief in the tenets of a given Jewish religious sect. As Dr. Davie and others have said, a Jew is still a Jew until he has sloughed off the religion and the rest of the culture of the group. Gentiles and Jews who have given up their Jewish religion usually express this viewpoint.

It was in this popular sense that *Fortune* magazine used the term "Jew," in a survey published in its issue of February, 1936. From this report, it appears that only 3,500 of the 4,500,000 "Jews" in the United States are members of the Communist party. Congressional investigations of "Red" activities have also disclosed the minor part played by "Jews" in American Communist organizations. The most outstanding leaders of the Communist party in this country are neither members of Jewish sects nor otherwise identified with the Jewish people. They include: Earl Browder, William Z. Foster, Clarence Hathaway, James

Ford, Robert Minor, William Paterson, Harry Haywood, and Ella Reeve Bloor.

Despite the latitude given by the popular and scientific definition of "Jew," the unfairness of declaiming at length about "Communist Jews" is as great as that of speaking as though there is any appreciable number of "atheistic Jews." After all, the outstanding Jewish organizations have condemned Communism as well as Nazism and Fascism.

To justify his emphasis upon "Communist Jews," Father Coughlin—despite the facts given above and the official position of his church—has tried to prove that the Russian Soviet revolution was a "Russian-Jewish Revolution." In his speech of November 20th, he asserted:

> Moreover, I have before me a quotation from the periodical named *The American Hebrew* of September 10, 1920, which says: "The achievement—the Russian-Jewish Revolution— destined to figure in history as the overshadowing result of the World War, was largely the outcome of Jewish thinking, of Jewish discontent, of Jewish effort to reconstruct."

The words, "the Russian-Jewish Revolution," are not in the article in *The American Hebrew*. The article was written by Svetozar Tonjoroff, a non-Jew, and is entitled, "Jews in World Reconstruction."

Rev. William C. Kernan, Rector of Trinity Episcopal Church, Bayonne, New Jersey, on December 4th, analyzed this Coughlin attack on the Jews thus:

> (The article) is significant for stating exactly the opposite of that which Father Coughlin made it appear to say. It does not use the phrase "Russian Jewish Revolution" at all—anywhere. It was not written by a Jew. It was written by a non-Jew. It asks the question, will the world follow the course that led to its blood-bath in 1914 or will it "adopt some principle approach-

ing the Golden Rule as the basis of its political and economic statesmanship"? It goes on to point out that "the Golden Rule, as too many of non-Jews are too apt to forget, is a Jewish principle. It is the expression of a Jewish discontent with social, economic and political conditions that existed in Palestine and in the world 19 centuries ago." It points out that the unrest caused by the Golden Rule, formulated through Jewish lips in Christ's Sermon on the Mount, finally resulted in the "annihilation of the most firmly entrenched, the most selfish and most reckless autocratic system in the world, Russian Czarism." *This* is what the author meant as being "largely the outcome of Jewish thinking, of Jewish discontent, of Jewish effort to reconstruct." The fall of the Czar. That was not caused by the Bolshevik Revolution. That was caused by the Kerensky Revolution—a revolution in which the Grand Duke Michael figured to become regent—a revolution supported by the Allies —a revolution commended by Theodore Roosevelt—a revolution that occurred in March, 1917—and a revolution which was itself overthrown by the Bolshevik Revolution in November 17, 1917. Father Coughlin did not tell us that. In other words the article in *The American Hebrew* did not say that the Communist Revolution was the outcome largely of "Jewish thinking, of Jewish discontent, of Jewish effort to reconstruct."

In spite of these facts, Father Coughlin went on in his November 20th speech to use the expression, "this effort to reconstruct society by means of Communism," clearly a distortion of the article.

The Catholic historian, Father Moody, whom we quote above, in his booklet on *Why are Jews Persecuted?* indicates the relatively insignificant role of "Jews" in the Soviet—the second Russian—revolution in the following passages:

Was not Marx, the founder of communism, a Jew? And is this not proof of the connection of the Jews with this dangerous doctrine? Marx was a Jew in the sense that he was born of Jewish parents. At the age of six he was baptized a Lutheran, and from that time on he had no connection whatever with Judaism. In fact, he cordially detested the Jews for their bourgeois spirit and considered them bulwarks of capitalism. . . .

Trotsky, . . . a Jew by birth, was visited by a delegation of rabbis and Jewish laymen in the early days of the revolution in Russia and was asked to disassociate himself from a cause that was bringing untold suffering to Jewry. His answer was: "Go home to your Jews and tell them that I am not a Jew, and I care nothing for the Jews and their fate." Now it seems to me extremely unfair to blame the Jews as a whole for the actions of these renegade members of their flock. Can you imagine our indignation if someone attacked us for the activities of an Azana or a Cardenas, both of whom are baptized Catholics? [1]

It is also interesting to note that while Marx was a Jew by birth, the intellectual progenitors of the founder of communism were not. Marx was not an original thinker; he borrowed from a variety of sources and merely voiced in a more systematic manner a rather widespread protest against the evils of the industrial system. Most of the elements of his doctrine had already been expressed by such men as Hegel, Feuerbach, Owen, Saint-Simon, Proudhon, Blanc, and Fourier. Not one of these was a Jew. The same is true of the spiritual fathers of Bolshevism. In that long list of men who prepared the Russian mind for the acceptance of the present order we look in vain for a member of this particular oppressed group. This is important, for the Soviet phenomenon is not pure Marxism; it is very definitely conditioned by the Russian mentality, and it owes as much to Lenin and other non-Jewish Russians as it does to Marx. . . .

The Jews as a whole had no love for the Czarist *régime,*

[1] And he might have added Hitler and Mussolini, both nominal Roman Catholics; and Stalin who was educated for the priesthood in the Greek Orthodox Catholic Church.

and most of them were to be found in the parties of the opposition, the constitutional democrats or the social-democrats. The Socialist Party in Russia before the revolution included only sixty thousand of the five million Jews, while the number of Jews in the Bolshevist group was negligible. While the revolution of March, 1917, which overthrew the czar, was welcomed by the Russian Jews, most of them resisted the Bolshevist attack in November against the provisional government. All three Jewish worker organizations declared against the new movement; the opposition of the Jewish middle class, who saw themselves ruined by the communist experiment, was even more pronounced.

In his *Antisemitism, Historically and Critically Examined,* Professor Valentin—quoted previously—expresses similar conclusions. The following sentences from his book are particularly pertinent:

Before the World War, the number of Jewish Bolsheviks was insignificant. Trotsky himself did not turn Bolshevik till 1917. Even in 1922, that is, after several years of intensive Bolshevising, the Jewish element only amounted to 19,526 members, or 5.2 per cent of the party, in spite of the fact that the Jews, in contrast to the rest of the Russian population, were very largely composed of town-dwellers, who were able to read and thus more accessible to propaganda.

What are the attitudes of leading Jews and Jewish organizations on political and economic issues? From the foregoing, it is evident that the overwhelming majority of the Jews are conservative in both politics and economics. In this country, they are Republicans or Democrats. Their attitude has been summarized briefly by the Jewish War Veterans of the United States, an organization with about 60,000 members. An editorial in the *Jewish Veteran* of March, 1938, states that the "J.W.V., in common with all veterans and patriotic organizations, is uncompromisingly opposed to Communism, Nazism, Fascism, and every other ism that conflicts in the slightest way with Americanism and democracy." Similar positions have been expressed, for example, by the B'nai B'rith, a national fraternal society; by the Jewish Labor Committee; and by the Central Conference of American Rabbis.

Is "internationalism" fairly used as a "bad name," synonymous with Communism? Another quotation from the Coughlin speech of November 20, 1938, will emphasize the use he makes of this word and idea:

> I say to the good Jews of America, be not indulgent with the irreligious atheistic Jews 🏷️ and Gentiles 🏷️ who promote the cause of persecution in the land of the Communists; the same ones who promote the cause of atheism 🏷️ in America. Be not lenient with your high financiers 🏷️ and politicians 🏷️ who assisted at the birth of the only political, social and economic system in all civilization that adopted atheism 🏷️ as its religion, internationalism 🏷️ as its patriotism, and slavery 🏷️ as its liberty.

This Name Calling and Card Stacking overlooks the good aspects of "internationalism," the aspects that are treasured in our religious, political, and social life. The Roman Catholic Church, for example, carries on the internationalist teachings of Christ Himself. As Pope Pius XI said on July 28, 1938:

> We regard racism and exaggerated nationalism as barriers raised between man and man, between people and people, between nation and nation. . . . All men are, above all, members of the same great kind. They all belong to the single great family of the living. Humankind is therefore a single, universal, catholic race.

In short, Father Coughlin's racism and opposition to all internationalism flouts the teachings of the religion he professes and of the late head of his church.

Jews have wandered over the face of the earth, frequently driven by persecution from their long-established homes, but their international-mindedness is of the same sort as that of Christians. Jews aid their co-religionists in Europe at times just as Christian Americans have aided all sorts of oppressed, starved, and otherwise destitute Christians, Jews, Chinese, etc., in all parts of the world. The American Friends' Service Committee has been pre-eminent in this sort of humanitarian work. The name and fame of the American Red Cross has thus been carried to all countries as a synonym for merciful ministrations to the victims of catastrophes. Both Catholics and Protestants, too, send American missionaries far and wide to carry the word of God as they see it.

The fact that Communists and Nazis, too, for that matter, also advocate a kind of international penetration, a kind quite different from that of the Protestants, Catholics, and Jews, quite different from that taught by Christ, is certainly no reason for making of "internationalism" a hateful name.

In other words, "internationalism" must be distorted to make it synonymous with Communism. Jews, Catholics, and Protestants all oppose Communism, but they all advocate peaceful, humanitarian internationalism. The term, "international Jew," therefore, should either be used in a complimentary way as similar to "international Christian" or be regarded as an effort to bring unjust reproach against Jewish religionists.

Westbrook Pegler, whose "Fair Enough" column appears in the New York *World-Telegram* and other papers,

a Roman Catholic himself, likes to contrast the internationalist activities of the Irish Catholics with those of the
Jews—to the benefit of the Jews and the confusion of
Father Coughlin. On March 21, 1939, he stated that "it
was particularly unbecoming of Father Coughlin to incite
bigotry, not only because he is an American and a priest
but also because Irish immigrants to this country in the last
century—from whom he sprang—were hated and persecuted for their religion and blood." Using the Catholic
history book, *Has the Emigrant Kept the Faith?*, written
by Professor Gerald O'Shaughnessy of Marist College,
Washington, D. C., Pegler recalls the "riots, often with
destruction of churches, in Providence, Cincinnati, New
Orleans, Dorchester, Roxbury, Charlestown, Lawrence,
Chelsea, Manchester, Bath, Norwalk, Brooklyn, Sauger-
ties, Palmyra, in Sydney and Massillon, Ohio, and Galves-
ton." Election Day, 1855, was made memorable as Bloody
Monday in Louisville because of Know-Nothing violence.

In his daily column of February 23, 1939, Pegler also
recalled the efforts of Irish-Americans to invade Canada
with armed troops on several occasions, etc., and that con-
cludes:

The American natives didn't like this any more than Father
Coughlin now likes the Jewish propaganda against the Nazis.
But Americans of Irish descent to this day can make out a case
for the immigrant plotters and fighters against the bloody op-
pressors in Ireland and for the sale of various issues of Kathleen
Mavourneen bonds for various Irish republics among American
citizens. Yet if the international Irish had been handled as
Father Coughlin's political comrades today propose to handle
Jews who are similarly international, this country might have
been denied the spiritual and intellectual benefit of his counsel.
That is something to think about one way or another.

The foregoing analysis of Father Coughlin's "bad names" is not all-inclusive. The facts given regarding his unfairness in speaking of "atheistic Jews," "Communist Jews," and "international Jews," however, indicate clearly the methods he uses in applying the Name Calling Device. With Father Coughlin's condemnation of Communism and with his apparent condemnation of Nazism, few in the United States would quarrel. But our analysis reveals the sorts of practice against which listeners must guard in his rhetorical barrages as well as in the talks and writings of other rabble-rousers. Even such generally accepted "bad names" as Nazism must be suspect. In this case, Father Coughlin rejects Nazism on the one hand and then advocates such undemocratic and fascistic measures as the use of "bullets instead of ballots" and the establishment of a "democratic Corporate State." In short, we must beware of omnibus words—to repeat—good or bad.

A fitting close for this chapter is the following list of outstanding persons whom Father Coughlin has attacked, whom he has called bad names, with a reference to one newspaper story in each case reporting such an attack:

Bernard M. Baruch, *Times*, March 12, 1935

William P. Bonbright, *Herald Tribune*, August 27, 1936

Robert J. Bulkley, *Times*, May 8, 1935

Josephus Daniels, *Times*, December 23, 1934

Norman H. Davis, *Times*, January 27, 1935

David Dubinsky, *Times*, September 12, 1936

DuPont family, *Times*, December 16, 1934

Mordecai Ezekiel, *World-Telegram*, August 28, 1936

Felix Frankfurter, *World-Telegram*, August 28, 1936

Carter Glass, *Times*, February 24, 1935

Herbert Hoover, *Times*, August 2, 1936
Hugh S. Johnson, *World-Telegram*, March 12, 1935
Alfred M. Landon, *Times*, August 1, 1936
Herbert H. Lehman, *Times*, July 25, 1936
J. P. Morgan, *Herald Tribune*, August 27, 1936
Henry Morgenthau, *Times*, October 24, 1936
Frank Murphy, *Herald Tribune*, March 21, 1936
William Henry, Cardinal O'Connell, *Times*, December 9, 1934
John J. O'Connor, *Times*, October 30, 1936
Frances Perkins, *Times*, September 12, 1936
James A. Reed, *Times*, November 4, 1934
Joseph T. Robinson, *Times*, January 30, 1935
John D. Rockefeller, *Herald Tribune*, August 27, 1936
Franklin D. Roosevelt, *Times*, September 26, 1936
Upton Sinclair, *Times*, October 28, 1934
Robert F. Wagner, *Post*, May 9, 1935
Henry A. Wallace, *Times*, September 26, 1936
James P. Warburg, *Times*, October 24, 1936
Woodrow Wilson, *Times*, December 23, 1934

Only one New York newspaper reference is given for each, for the sake of brevity, although Father Coughlin has repeatedly attacked many of these men and the stories have appeared in many other newspapers.

This list speaks for itself. It contains revered leaders from many walks of American life.

Glittering Generality—associating something with a "virtue word"—is used to make us accept and approve the thing without examining the evidence.

V. Glittering Generality

WE BELIEVE in, fight for, live by "virtue words" about which we have deep-set ideas. Such words are "civilization," "Christianity," "good," "proper," "right," "democracy," "patriotism," "motherhood," "fatherhood," "science," "medicine," "health," and "love."

For our purposes in propaganda analysis, we call these "virtue words" Glittering Generalities in order to focus attention upon this dangerous characteristic that they have: *They mean different things to different people; they can be used in different ways.*

This is not a criticism of these words as we understand them. Quite the contrary. *It is a criticism of the uses to which propagandists put the cherished words and beliefs of unsuspecting people.*

When someone talks to us about "democracy," we immediately think of our own definite ideas about democracy, the ideas we learned at home, at school, and in church. Our first and natural reaction is to assume that the speaker is using the word in our sense, that he believes as we do on this important subject. This lowers our "sales resistance" and makes us far less suspicious than we ought to be when the speaker begins telling us the things "the United

States *must do* to preserve democracy." If we have permitted our "sales resistance" to be lowered by the use of
"democracy" as a Glittering Generality rather than as a
carefully defined term, we may soon find ourselves being
"sold" such an anti-democratic notion as a "Corporate
State" under a "democratic" disguise, one of Father
Coughlin's tricks.

The Glittering Generality is, in short, Name Calling in
reverse. While Name Calling seeks to make us form a
judgment to *reject and condemn* without examining the
evidence, the Glittering Generality device seeks to make us
approve and accept without examining the evidence. In
acquainting ourselves with the Glittering Generality Device, therefore, all that has been said regarding Name Calling must be kept in mind, and especially should we remember what has been said about *omnibus words*.

Propagandists are most effective in the use of both of
these devices when their words can make us create devils
to fight or gods to adore. By their use of "bad words," we
may be led to personify as a "devil" some nation, race,
group, individual, policy, practice, or ideal; we may be
made fighting mad to destroy it. By their use of "good
words," we may be led to personify as a godlike idol some
nation, race, group, or the like. Before we are led to any
such position, we should know what the propagandist is
trying to do with us. If we are to be led, we should be led
with our eyes open, not blindly.

In analyzing a Glittering Generality, we must ask ourselves such questions as these and suspend judgment until
we have answered them:

What does the "virtue word" really mean?
Does the idea in question—the proposal of the propagandist

—have a legitimate connection with the real meaning of the name?

Is an idea that does not serve my best interests and the best interests of society, as I see them, being "sold" to me merely through its being given a name that I like?

In other words, leaving the "virtue word" out of consideration, what are the merits of the idea itself?

Father Coughlin's Glittering Generalities. In this as in the preceding chapter, space does not permit us to analyze all the specific words and ideas Father Coughlin has used and misused in the present fashion. Nor is it necessary. Only some of his chief Glittering Generalities are here subjected to scientific scrutiny in order to illustrate and assess his applications of the device. The following Coughlin "virtue words" have been selected as examples:

1. "Americanism" and "democracy."
2. "Rightist," as a label for the political position of Jefferson, Washington, and other leading advocates of democracy.
3. "German citizen Jews," "good Jews," "religious Jews."
4. "Defense mechanism," a term he uses as descriptive of the relationship between Nazism and Communism, Communism and the old "economic system."

It is not necessary to add to these the title of his magazine, *Social Justice.* From the analysis of our examples, the strange meanings he gives "social" and "justice" become abundantly clear. This analysis also suggests the uses to which he puts such other "virtue words" as "Christian," "our better sympathies," "liberty," etc.

It should be noted at the outset that Father Coughlin, like most propagandists who make a strong appeal to emotions, frequently combines the Name Calling and Glittering Generality Devices to obtain a sharp alignment of sympathies, a sharp clash of conflicting emotions. Rev. Walton E. Cole, minister of the First Unitarian Church of Toledo, Ohio, emphasized this point on March 24, 1939, in "An Analysis of Father Coughlin's Techniques" before the Institute of Arts and Sciences at Columbia University. Reverend Cole said:

> Like all propagandists he over-simplifies. Everything is black or white, for God or for the devil. . . .
>
> He likes to speak of a "contest between Christ and chaos!" He wants you to feel that you must be "either with us or against us. You can't be indifferent."

Let us look at our examples:

1. *"Americanism" and "democracy"*: The first amendment to the Federal Constitution echoed the revolt of our Ulster Scots, Scots, Germans, Irish, Huguenots, Quakers, and others, against government control of religion, against the royal licensing of the press, against the Star Chamber and the pillory, etc. The first amendment is as follows:

> Congress shall make no law respecting an establishment of religion, or prohibiting the free exercise thereof; or abridging the freedom of speech or of the press; or the right of the people peaceably to assemble and to petition the government for redress of grievances.

The fourteenth amendment has been interpreted by the Supreme Court as making these provisions binding upon the States. These provisions are also indelibly identified in the minds of Americans as principles essential to Americanism and democracy.

Father Coughlin speaks well of democracy. On January 9, 1938, for instance, he asserted:

> I maintain that as American citizens, we should pledge ourselves singly and unitedly to cease sniping at our democratic

form of government ❖. Why blame democracy ❖ for the condition in which we find ourselves? Preferably, let us blame a lack of democracy ❖ which at one time pandered to plutocracy and, at a later date, flirted with Fascism and collaborated with Communism and its class warfare.

Despite the patience of Americans with his activities, too, Father Coughlin has tried to make much of his difficulties in obtaining radio time for his speeches and in developing the circulation of his magazine, *Social Justice*.

Despite his unusual freedom, in view of what he preaches, and despite his lip-service to democracy, this man makes such statements as the following, an extract from his talk of January 1, 1939:

Our people are told incessantly that Communism is a form of democracy ❖, that Fascism and Nazism are outright tyrannies; but Americans are seldom warned that both these un-American forms of government must be stamped out peremptorily. They are seldom advised that the free speech ❖ of the Communist or the free speech of the Nazi may not be used to destroy the free speech ❖ of the American. In the face of all this, I ask you calmly, what of Americanism ❖ and our democracy ❖? Is there no one to defend them?

In other words *Father Coughlin attempts to praise "Americanism" and "free speech" and at the same instant to demand that we violate the Constitutional guarantee of free speech.* For all his verbal flag-waving, he is asking us to violate one of the most cherished principles of democracy!

Contrary to what Father Coughlin asserts, our people are told incessantly by our politicians, newspapers, radio commentators, magazines, etc., that Communism, Fascism and Nazism are *all* outright tyrannies. We are frequently warned that these un-American forms of government must not be permitted to gain any headway in the United States, and we have therefore and because of our experience with democratic processes placed scant credence in Communism, Fascism, or Nazism.

It is true that Americans are seldom advised that the free speech of the Communist or the free speech of the Nazi should not be "used to destroy" the free speech of the American. But this is because we as a people believe that the free speech of the Communist and the Nazi can do us no harm. It was because of just such a belief that "Congress shall make no law . . . abridging the freedom of speech or of the press," nor may other American law-making bodies.

Not satisfied with demanding the violation of our traditional and legal freedom of speech in a number of his 1938-1939 addresses, Father Coughlin has also trod upon another sacred American right, *freedom of religion*. On several occasions, *he has attacked American political institutions for not making more definite efforts to establish religion in our schools and elsewhere*. For "religion" he has his own definition. In his talk of December 18, 1938, Father Coughlin put this proposition in this form:

Once more, nations will either reassert their belief in the supernatural Messias (Messiah) and the supernatural order of life ❀ which He instituted, or they will complete their rejection of Him, logically proceeding to exterminate Him in the personal life of the individual.

For it is untenable to retain, side by side, the individual doctrine ❀ of Christ and the social doctrine of anti-Christ. I characterize this position as untenable because Christ, the Messias (Messiah), must be accepted as such both in our individual and social lives, which are so intimately intermingled that only with great difficulty can they be separated in practice.

But the Federal Constitution's first amendment says: "Congress shall make no law respecting an establishment of religion, or prohibiting the free exercise thereof." Father Coughlin is using, in substance, the same arguments that were once employed to support the establishment of one sect as a state church in England, Scotland, and Ireland, in various continental countries, and even in such American colonies as Massachusetts and Connecticut. These are the arguments against which our ancestors rebelled, a rebellion that culminated in the inclusion of the guarantee of freedom for *any* religion—Catholic, Jewish, Latter-day Saint, agnostic, Jehovah's Witness, Presbyterian, Unitarian, Friend, Mohammedan, atheist, Buddhist, or any other—in the Federal Constitution.

Our ancestors who rebelled against the dictation of their religious beliefs by a political régime wanted to make certain that in the United States religion would be a *personal* and not a *national* affair. If we should begin to narrow our definition of religion, we might once again reach the stage where only Presbyterians, Methodists, Catholics, or some other faith would be called "religious," and all others would be classed as "atheists," "heretics," or "pagans." In the history of all too many of our faiths are the records of the stake, the rack, the pillory, and the ducking stool, the prices the faithful have paid at other times or in other countries for disagreement with an established religion.

What does Father Coughlin mean, too, by "the social doctrine of anti-Christ"? Why does he say that nations permitting religious freedom, nations that take no official position on "belief in the supernatural Messias (Messiah) and the supernatural order of social life He instituted"—why does he say that such nations "will complete their rejection of Him, logically proceeding to exterminate Him in the personal life of the individual"? The experience of Americans with democracy—as democracy is defined in our Federal Constitution—indicates no such results. The bad names, "anti-Christ" and "heretic," have too often been used to condemn without question all but the orthodox religious views of one sect. They have been applied to Quakers, Roman Catholics, Baptists, Unitarians, Methodists, agnostics, and others as well as to admitted atheists. Father Coughlin has trod on dangerous ground when he calls for the violation of religious freedom. No cloak of "Americanism" or "democracy" should be permitted to disguise his apparent purposes.

Other examples of Father Coughlin's use of "Americanism" and "democracy" as Glittering Generalities are frequent in his speeches and writings. They include his preachings of distrust and even hatred for our legally elected representatives and administrators, for the democratic functioning of our labor unions, and for the racial and ethnic minorities within our frontiers. The two cases we give in some detail, however, suffice to illustrate the extremes to which he goes, the methods he utilizes.

2. *"Rightist" as a label for the political position of Jefferson, Washington, and other leading advocates of democracy:* In his speech of January 15, 1939, Father Coughlin expounded this theory of political groupings: A small group of "Leftists," who call themselves "Liberals," actively promote the cause of the centralization of power in the hands of the Federal Government. A much smaller group of "Rightists," whom Father Coughlin identified as "Conservatives," "Reactionaries," and "sincere believers in democracy," actively promote "democracy." Between these two militant groups, in the political

scale, are the great mass of Americans, whom he calls "Indifferentists."

Under "Leftist," Coughlin groups all those who believe in Communism, Nazism, Fascism, New-Dealism, and "majority rule"!

This line-up is so absurd that it scarcely requires analysis. Only by the most obvious distortion of the term could Thomas Jefferson—the enemy of the *status quo*—be called a "Conservative." An ardent Whig, one of the chief authors of that revolutionary document, the Declaration of Independence, and one of the strongest advocates of the Bill of Rights, Jefferson was classed by his conservative contemporaries as a radical. They were gravely concerned when he was elected President of the United States. Both Jefferson and Washington believed in "majority rule," but Washington was on the Federalist or strong-central-government side of the state-national struggle, the opposite from Jefferson. Father Coughlin calls both of these men "Rightists."

Traditionally, the terms Leftist and Rightist are assigned quite different meanings. *Webster's New International Dictionary*, an authority on American usage, defines the "Left" as the members of a European legislature who have seats on the left of the chamber, an indication of membership in a liberal, radical, or democratic party. A member of the Left or a Leftist is, therefore, a liberal, a radical, or a democrat, one who fights against the "vested interests." Similarly, Rightists are "conservatives" or "monarchists," those who uphold the privileges of the "vested interests," especially of vested property interests.

What is Father Coughlin's apparent purpose in assigning such new and strong definitions to these traditional terms? The rest of his speech of January 15 makes his purpose quite clear. The explanation lies, however, not on this but on the other side of the Atlantic. By common consent, the Rebel armies of General Francisco Franco were labeled the Rightists. This was in line with the traditional definition of the word because Franco had the backing of the monarchists, the old royal army leaders, and others who have or had a strong vested interest in the *status quo* of before the revolt. The Spaniards who sided with the Spanish government were also by common consent called the Leftists because of their liberal, radical, and democratic leanings. We are not taking sides in this conflict, as does Father Coughlin; we are merely stating the situation as it is understood and accepted in the United States.

On Father Coughlin's crusade to help the Spanish Rightists, including his efforts to keep the Federal Government from lifting its arms embargo against the Spanish Leftists, he wanted to identify Franco's position with that of our most revered American political leaders. Regardless of the merits of Franco's case, the scientific analyst of propaganda has his suspicions aroused by this distortion of Glittering Generalities to suit a propagandist's own purposes.

3. *"German citizen Jews," "good Jews," "religious Jews":* Father Coughlin's use of the terms, "good Jews" and "religious Jews," is always in contrast with his "bad names," "bad Jews" and "atheistic Jews." As the preceding chapter proves, the apparent intent of these terms is to indicate that all too many Jews are not "good" and "religious," an unfair attack on such a conservative and religious people. Father Coughlin's use of these Glittering Generalities is a continuation of his acceptance of the Nazi myth of a Jewish "race" or at least "nation," concepts re-

jected by scientists and by the official spokesmen for the Roman Catholic Church. If he wished to avoid direct accusation of Jew-baiting, he would not have had any need for such terms as "good Jews" and "religious Jews" at all. After all, he does not speak of "good Protestants" and "bad Protestants," "good Catholics" and "bad Catholics."

The Glittering Generality, "German citizen Jews," raises a more serious criticism of Father Coughlin's methods. In his speech of November 20, 1938, he makes the following statements (italics ours):

Although cruel persecution of German-born Jews has been notorious since 1933, *particularly in the loss of their citizenship*, nevertheless until last week the Nazi purge was concerned chiefly with foreign-born Jews. German citizen Jews ⁑ were not molested officially in the conduct of their business. The property of German citizen Jews ⁑ was not confiscated by the government although a few synagogues and stores were destroyed by mob violence. The children of German citizen Jews ⁑ were permitted to attend public schools with other children. The German citizen Jewish bankers ⁑ pursued their business as usual. The German citizen Rabbis ⁑ were permitted the practice of their rites, although recently some of their synagogues have been raided. Until this hour no German citizen Jew ⁑ has been martyred for his religion by government order, although restrictions were placed upon Jews professionally. While it is true that foreign-citizen Jews resident in Germany were disparaged and expelled, it is likewise true that many social impediments were placed in the pathway of Catholics and Protestants by the Nazi government—impediments which are revolting to our American concepts of liberty ⁑.

Father Coughlin admits that the Jews were deprived of German citizenship, a result of the so-called Nuremberg Laws promulgated in September, 1935. He then insists upon the relative freedom from "official" persecution enjoyed by a *non-existent group*, the "German citizen Jews."

Let us set aside, for the moment, this Glittering Generality and examine the evidence.

Goering, frequently alluded to as the "No. 2 Nazi" by informed observers, stated the official Nazi position with regard to Jews as follows in a speech delivered on March 10, 1933:

> The police are not a defense squad for Jewish stores. . . . They tell me I must call out the police to protect them (the Jews). Certainly, I shall employ the police, and without mercy, wherever German people are hurt, but I refuse to turn the police into a guard for Jewish stores. . . . The Nation is aroused. For years we told the people, "You can settle accounts with the traitors." We stand by our word. Accounts are being settled.

The files of any daily newspaper in the United States carry adequate reports of the consequences of this brutal position. In his own words, Goering places the full responsibility for this incredible record upon the present German government and its counterpart, the Nazi Party.

Let us look quite briefly at this record of Nazi horror. A brief summary indicates clearly the extent to which Father Coughlin's statements—if they are meant to refer to German-born Jews—distort the facts.

James G. McDonald, in a letter to the League of Nations resigning as High Commissioner for Refugees (of all kinds), dated December 27, 1935, reported as follows on the situation in Germany up to that time:

> The facts which arouse these apprehensions are indisputable. They are evidenced clearly in the German laws, decrees, judicial decisions and Party pronouncements and practices during

the last two years. The culmination of these attacks on the Jews, the Christian "non-Aryans," and the political and religious dissenters was the new legislation announced at the Party Congress at Nuremberg last September. The core of that enactment was the law limiting citizenship to those who are of "German or cognate Blood," and who also conform to the National Socialist conception of loyalty to the State. As the direct result in Germany not only the Jews, who now number about 435,000, but also tens of thousands of Christian "non-Aryans" who are classified as Jews, lost their citizenship, were disfranchised, and made ineligible to hold public office. Indirectly, through this new law, a constitutional basis was laid for unrestricted discriminations against all those whom the Party may wish to penalize.

The denationalization by the German government of thousands of German citizens has added to the hardships both of those remaining in Germany and of the refugees, and is an increasing burden on States which have admitted the refugees while in possession of German nationality. . . .

Relentlessly the Jews and "non-Aryans" are excluded from all public offices, from the exercise of the liberal professions, and from any part in the cultural and intellectual life of Germany. Ostracized from social relations with "Aryans," they are subjected to every kind of humiliation. Neither sex nor age exempts them from discrimination. Even the Jewish and "non-Aryan" children do not escape cruel forms of segregation and persecution. In Party publications, directly sponsored by the Government, "Aryan" children are stirred to hate the Jews and the Christian "non-Aryans," to spy upon them and to attack them, and to incite their own parents to extirpate the Jews altogether. . . .

It is being made increasingly difficult for Jews and "non-Aryans" in Germany to sustain life. Condemned to segregation within the four corners of the legal and social Ghetto which has now closed upon them, they are increasingly prevented from earning their living. Indeed more than half the Jews remaining in Germany have already been deprived of their livelihood. In many parts of the country there is a systematic attempt at starvation of the Jewish population. In no field of economic activity is there any security whatsoever. For some time it has been impossible for Jewish businessmen and shop-keepers to carry on their trades in small towns. The campaign against any dealings with Jews is now systematically prosecuted in the larger towns, despite the restrictions upon migration from the provinces into the few largest cities where Jewish economic activity is not yet completely excluded. The Jews are fleeing to those cities because there only can they hope to escape, at least for a time, from the more brutal forms of persecution.

But the conditions Mr. McDonald describes, as difficult as they were for the Jews, were mild contrasted with what followed. The *World Almanac* for 1939 calls the Nazi persecutions of November, 1938, "a wave of destruction, looting and incendiarism unparalleled in Germany since the Thirty Years' War." The civilized world was shocked. Such outstanding Americans as President F. D. Roosevelt, ex-President Herbert Hoover, Alfred M. Landon, Alfred E. Smith, Rev. Robert L. Gannon, President of Fordham University, and Bishop Edwin H. Hughes of the Methodist Episcopal Church expressed their horror and condemnation.

The Manchester *Guardian Weekly*, December 2, 1938, gives a brief sketch of the wave of incidents that made civilized peoples recoil, as follows:

A growing mass of evidence shows that the anti-Semitic excesses in Germany have been far worse than they seemed at first, even in Berlin. And, fearful as they were in Berlin, they have been even worse in other German cities, especially Vienna.

The treatment of Jews in the concentration camps has been terrible all along, but since the assassination of Herr vom Rath it has been almost beyond description, especially in the camps at Buchenwald and Sachsenhausen. There a multitude of Jews has been murdered by Nazis, some being shot and others being done to death with blows from spades, cudgels, and so on.

Only a few Jewish shops in Vienna survived the "Anschluss," but when Herr vom Rath was assassinated even these were closed, although all the shop assistants were "Aryans" and are now unemployed. In the excesses that followed neither the aged nor the crippled were spared. Two cases have come to my knowledge. One, an old man who had been lame for ten years, was so badly beaten by Nazis that he became a complete cripple. When he knew that he would never walk again he committed suicide. The other had only one leg and was so badly beaten by Nazis that it was rendered useless. He is now in a very critical condition.

The most horrible part of the anti-Semitic excesses in Vienna is that the Nazis deliberately smashed Jewish noses. There are about 1,000 Jews in Viennese hospitals now suffering from injuries inflicted by gangs of S.A., and S.S., and of these about 300 have badly broken noses.

Thousands of Viennese Jews are homeless—many have been burnt or smoked out of their homes,—and thousands are in prison or confined in small rooms. These rooms are packed with Jews, who are crowded together so tightly that there is hardly space for them to sit, still less to lie down. An Englishman who visited one of these dens declared that the "Black Hole of Calcutta was nothing by comparison."

The police look on helplessly while Jews are ill-treated in the streets. Men and women, both old and young, are treated with the same indignity. Elderly men have been forced to crawl along the streets on their bellies, wearing nothing but their pants. Refined Jewish women are forced to clean the latrines of the S.A. and S.S. Non-Jews are, as a rule, too frightened to help the Jews or even sell them goods. Innumerable Jewish women and children do not know what has happened to fathers, husbands, and sons. Many Jews arrested in Vienna have been sent to the concentration camps at Dachau.

The foregoing makes apparent the extent to which Father Coughlin's statements minimize the shocking sequence of events. It indicates the unfair trickery in such a meaningless term as "German citizen Jews" and in his Card Stacking contrast between "official" actions and "mob violence."

4. *"Defense mechanism," a term Coughlin uses as descriptive of the relationship between Nazism and Communism, Communism and the old "economic system":* In the preceding chapter, we reduced to simple statements Father Coughlin's theory of the rise of Nazism and its persecution complex. This theory, in brief, traces the rise of Nazism, by the way of Communism, back to "the greed of the money changers." "Bad Jews and Gentiles," Father Coughlin asserts, were "the money changers, who persecuted, then pilloried the teeming populations of Europe." Against them, "atheistic Jews and Gentiles" constructed Communism as a "defense mechanism." Communism, in turn, persecuted Catholics and Protestants but not—Father Coughlin inaccurately alleges—Jews. As a "defense mechanism" against Communism, Father Coughlin then claims, Hitler and his followers created Nazism and proceeded to persecute Jews, Catholics, and Protestants.

This theory is fundamental to Father Coughlin's recent propaganda. Despite its logical inconsistencies and its neglect and distortion of well-authenticated historical evidence, he has repeated it directly and by inference a number of times. Above all else, in this theory Father Coughlin overlooks the fact that *the United States government recognized and lent money to democratic governments in both pre-Soviet and pre-Nazi Germany.* Democracy is the only "defense mechanism" against persecution that a democratic nation or people is willing to recognize as adequate. Father Coughlin does not agree.

Competent observers, including social scientists, who have analyzed the rise of Communism, are agreed on these points: The so-called Kerensky or democratic government of Russia, formed after the first or democratic revolution of 1917, was undermined by the Imperial German government in an effort to obtain from it a separate peace. The Imperial German government arranged for the passage of Lenin from exile in Switzerland through Germany and Sweden to Russia in order that this outstanding Bolshevik might lead a second—the Communist—revolution of 1917 in Russia. Ludendorf, later Hitler's ally, reports this in his memoirs. With few exceptions, the leaders of both the Kerensky and the Communist revolutions and governments were Gentiles, regardless of whether we accept the scientific or the Hitler definition of that term. Evidence in this connection is presented later in the chapter on Card Stacking.

Father Coughlin's acceptance of the Hitler theory that Nazism is a "defense mechanism" against Communism stirred up a wave of enthusiastic approval for Coughlin's November 20 speech throughout the Nazi press. Otto D. Tolischus, a special correspondent at Berlin for the New York *Times,* reported this reaction in a dispatch printed on November 27, 1938, as follows:

The German hero in America for the moment is the Rev. Charles E. Coughlin because of his radio speech representing national socialism as a defensive front against bolshevism.

American sympathizers with Nazism chimed in. William D. Pelley, leader of the Silver Shirts, an organization devoted to the cause of driving Jews from American life, asserted in his magazine, *Liberation:*

This past week, the aggressive Father Coughlin went on the air over a New York radio station and delivered what amounted to the prize Silver Shirt speech of the year.

The official journal (*Deutscher Weckruf und Beobachter*) of the German-American Bund, Hitler's Nazi organization in the United States, saluted Father Coughlin on December 1, 1938, as the "heroic priest, one of the few outstanding Americans who has the courage of his convictions, and whom the Jews have not been able to intimidate."

But let us not be satisfied to reject Father Coughlin's "defense mechanism" theory in the case of Nazism because of Nazi enthusiasm for it. In this instance, as in all analyses of propagandas, the theory should stand or fall as a result of our examination of the facts. The Institute for Propaganda Analysis, Inc., has already published a study of the "Propaganda Techniques of German Fascism" as bulletin number 8 of *Propaganda Analysis*, Volume I. Pertinent passages in this bulletin are the following:

Germany's defeat in the World War and her humiliation in the Treaty of Versailles had become less significant in the reconstruction period of the Weimar Republic; but at the end of the Twenties the world depression struck the German people another crushing blow and brought unemployment and impoverishment to increasing millions. Anger and unrest filled the land. In such a period it was natural in Germany, as anywhere, that a large section of the population should lend a favorable ear to anyone who offered himself as a savior. The Socialists and Communists attributed the depression and its consequences to the inherent weaknesses of a system of production for private profit. This they sought to replace by a system of public ownership. Their program made a rational appeal; as propaganda, however, it was much less effective than the emotionally charged propaganda of the Nazis.

The program and, more particularly, the actions of the National Socialist party have reflected the frustrations and despairs of the German workers, farmers, and middle class. Hitler's life actually epitomized and dramatized the experiences of the German people. Until his final overwhelming political victory, Hitler had known only failure. He wanted to be an artist and failed; an architect, and became a house painter; he went into the war with all possible enthusiasm and returned from it a physical wreck with no hope and no future in the country which had lost. Some excuse, some outlet, had to be found.

The middle class, one of the most politically important sections of the population, had been neglected. After the war this class in particular suffered from Germany's failure, defeat and humiliation. It suffered from the failure of the Weimar Republic to cope effectively with the economic crisis.

It distrusted Communism. It feared violent change, but it wanted such change as would give a sense of security. Then came Adolf Hitler, a leader, who promised the people all that they wanted. Most Germans felt that conditions were too bad even to question how all that he offered could be achieved. The few who did raise their voices in protest or doubt were silenced by argument, by force, or by honest conviction that this new scheme, this new hope, must be tried. Everything was promised to everyone: socialism to the laborer and to the more liberal Kleinburger; partition of the great estates to the peasant; dissolution of trusts and economic security to the middle class citizen; salvation from communism to the upper bourgeois; and to everyone elimination of the Jews, rearmament of the Reich, and "national liberation." This was the appeal of the "National Socialist German Labor Party." A mass following was the result. Power, however, could come only by persuading the industrialists, the financiers, and the feudal military caste to support the Nazi movement. Hitler united them, organized them and won their support with his promises that they should not fear his labor-winning social program. It was understood that they could retain control behind the scenes if Hitler were left free to manage the political show.

It is difficult to estimate the support or strength of the industrialists. As in most countries many business leaders contributed to all the major parties. Despite its socialism, the growing following of the NSDAP made it a useful tool to crush Marxism, democracy, and the German labor movement. The list of industrialists and aristocratic contributors expanded rapidly between 1925 and 1933, especially after 1930. The most powerful figure was the Ruhr magnate, Chairman Fritz Thyssen of the Vereinigte Stahlwerke A. G. The importance of this financial backing, however, should not be overemphasized. So far as present records show, these men did not determine the policies of the party. Those had been decided before their support was elicited. "Socialism" was a Glittering Generality privately admitted by the party leaders. They had no plan and no intention of changing the existing economic system. Capitalism was all they knew and all they wanted. But once in power, political control dominated economic control.

"Capitalism," as free enterprise, became a Glittering Generality. Hitler, the master propagandist, knew that propaganda, to be effective, must be keyed to the desires, hopes, hatreds, loves, fears, and prejudices of the people; he knew that most human beings crave a scapegoat to take the blame of disaster and to bolster their own pride. The Jews were made the scapegoat. He blamed them not only for the existing unemployment and impoverishment but also for the loss of the war and the Treaty of Versailles. But the anti-Jewish propaganda had even greater value to Nazism than the mere creation of a scapegoat. Through the Jews Hitler was able to strike at anyone, Jew or non-Jew, opposed to Nazism, and to discredit any plan which aimed at the peaceful rehabilitation of Germany. Hitler's objective was to create in the minds of Germans an ugly image of "Jew." The word "Jew" was deliberately made synonymous with everything the Germans resented and hated or could be led to resent and hate. Once that was done, Nazi agitators revived or manufactured for circulation notorious forgeries, which branded all those persons as Jews who did or said anything not in accord with Nazi ideas. To attack the Dawes Plan, for example, it became necessary to label Dawes as a Jew and so, according to *Der Sturmer,* Dawes was portrayed to its readers as a full-blooded Jew, originally named Davidson. The banking house of J. P. Morgan, which acted as a house of issue for a German government loan opposed by Hitler, was promptly branded a Jewish banking house and the Morgan name given as an abridgment of the more Jewish-sounding Morganstern. Similarly the entire French nation, whom the Nazis consider to be Germany's natural enemy, was described as a nation of Jews.

The Germans, Hitler said, were the World's greatest race, supreme in the arts of peace and unconquerable in war unless betrayed by the Jews. Thus, he was able to give to the National Socialist program the driving power of strong nationalism, coupled with the emotional appeal of racial superiority, intensified by hatred of the despised Jews. At the same time he inveighed against the great bankers, industrialists, and land-owners as vigorously as did the Communists and Socialists. He proclaimed himself the savior of the farmers, the small business men, and the workers. As early as 1920 Hitler's newly created National Socialist party made promises identical with those of the Socialists and Communists. The NSDAP platform adopted in Munich, February 24, 1920, included these demands: abolition of unearned incomes, nationalization of all trusts, abolition of interest on land loans, the enactment of a law for confiscation without compensation of land for public purposes.

From this evidence, it is apparent that Nazism can no more be called a "defense mechanism" against Communism than can any other undemocratic program. *A physician gives his patient an antitoxin—not a worse disease—as a defense mechanism against an infection. Similarly, democratic leaders advocate means for making democracy work, means for checking political infections.* They do not glorify such a program as Nazism with such a Glittering Generality as "defense mechanism."

We have now illustrated with Father Coughlin's words the unfair applications of the two omnibus-word devices, Name Calling and Glittering Generality. Let us now turn to somewhat more complex devices, beginning with Transfer.

Transfer carries the authority, sanction, and prestige of something respected and revered over to something else in order to make the latter acceptable.

VI. Transfer

AT 4 o'clock, Sunday afternoon, December 11, 1938, we turn on our radio. It happens to be tuned to station WHBI, Newark, New Jersey.

Organ music—"Trees."

An announcer speaks with great solemnity thus:

Ladies and gentlemen: We present at this time the regular Sunday afternoon address of Father Charles E. Coughlin, from Royal Oak, Michigan. After you listen to the address of Father Coughlin, you are invited to write your comments to WHBI, Newark, New Jersey.

More churchlike music, from an organ.

Another announcer speaks in an equally solemn manner as follows:

Ladies and gentlemen: Once more it is my privilege to present to you Father Charles E. Coughlin, from the Shrine of the Little Flower, at Royal Oak, Michigan. He will speak to you this afternoon on a subject pertinent to persecution and Communism. . . .

Transcribed and directed by Mr. Enold Courteau of New York, the Little Flower Choristers will sing for you the Advent Hymn: "Oh come, oh come, Emmanuel." During the singing of this hymn, please 'phone some friend or family to listen to this program, which will be of outstanding interest to every American.

And then—following the beautiful hymn—comes a blast of intemperate oratory, alleged to be an "educational talk on economics and politics."

The chief Propaganda Device employed by Father Coughlin in the foregoing is not marked with a symbol. This whole introduction to his program, as condensed here, is an application of the Transfer Device. By Transfer he attempts to carry the authority, sanction and prestige of something respected and revered by millions (the Roman Catholic Church) over to something else (his own economic, political, and even racial views) that he wishes to make thus more acceptable to us.

In the application of the Transfer Device, symbols are constantly used. With the Cross, the propagandist lends the sanctity of the Christian religion to his program. The flag, standing for the nation and for patriotism, performs a similar service. Cartoonists make "Uncle Sam" portray an alleged consensus of public opinion. These symbols stir emotions. At their very sight, with the speed of light, is aroused the whole complex of feelings we have with respect to church or nation.

As in the case of Father Coughlin's Sunday afternoon programs, propagandists seldom permit a Transfer to depend upon one symbol. Music, pageantry, uniforms, ritual, scenery—all are studied and utilized when appropriate.

How can we analyze the Transfer Device, now that we know how to spot it? How can we distinguish its legitimate from its illegitimate—its fair from its unfair—application? We must teach ourselves to *suspend judgment* until we have answered these questions:

What is the proposal of the propagandist, stated as simply and concretely as possible?

What is the meaning of the thing from which the propagandist is seeking to Transfer authority, sanction, and prestige?

Is there any legitimate connection between the proposal of the propagandist and the respected and revered thing, person, or institution?

In other words, leaving the propagandistic trick out of the picture, what are the merits of the propagandist's proposal viewed alone?

To illustrate further Father Coughlin's applications of the Transfer Device, it is not necessary to belabor the uses to which he puts symbols of the authority, sanction, and prestige of Christianity and the Roman Catholic Church. Even though Father Coughlin's economic and political views have been discredited by Cardinal Mundelein, by the semi-official Vatican newspaper, and by other Roman Catholic leaders and periodicals—as we have shown elsewhere in this book—he continues to infuse all manner of religious symbolism into his Sunday afternoon talks. He even draws analogies between the persecution of Christ and the persecutions to which he says he is unjustly subjected. One further example, taken from his address of February 25, 1934, will suffice. In arguing for his scheme of "credits for all" in the "United States, Incorporated," Father Coughlin declaimed:

My friends, this is the most important crusade which we have ever undertaken.

Its result will be financial democracy or financial slavery.

It is a contest between Christ 🌑 and chaos. . . .

Under the symbol of His cross 🌑 are we organized to be our brothers' keeper.

That is why I ask each one of you to carry about in your pockets or in your purses this symbol of redemption 🌑 from slavery both here and hereafter; this symbol of brotherly love 🦟.

There is a crucifix in my office for you free for the asking if you will address a letter to me this week.

You are either with us or against us. You can't be indifferent.

This crucifix 🦟 is a symbol of credits for all, justice for all and love for all.

The chief other institution from which Father Coughlin seeks to Transfer authority, sanction, and prestige to his proposals is science. This Transfer was used particularly in his talk of November 20, 1938. As he said in the first of these speeches:

> Thus, in a spirit of mutual co-operation, in a scientific spirit of coldly facing causes in order to remove effects 🦟, let us pause to inquire why Nazism is so hostile to Jewry in particular, and how the Nazi quality of persecution can be liquidated.

Sprinkled through his other speeches are such other words summoning up the "science" Transfer as: "facts," "analyzing," "seek to discover," "evidence," etc.

Let us ask ourselves these questions regarding this Transfer: What is science? Are Father Coughlin's searches to "discover" "cause" and "effect" carried out in a "scientific spirit"?

Much has been and still can be written in answer to the question, What is science? On the general answer to this question, however, scientists are in agreement. Science, as John Fiske once wrote, "is simply common sense rectified, extended, and methodized." *Science places primary emphasis upon observations that have been made and verified by competent observers and that may be verified by other competent observers.* Scientific theories must accord with an extensive—an exhaustive—array of such observations or facts. When theories do not harmonize with new facts or when old observations necessary to the demonstration of a theory are shown to be faulty, the scientist is quite willing to discard or modify the theories. It is antithetical to the scientific spirit to neglect well-authenticated facts, and no one can be called scientific who distorts a fact either intentionally or through neglect of known evidence.

How, then, from the analyses presented in the preceding chapters as well as in those which follow, can Father Coughlin presume to call himself "scientific"? Fact after fact in Father Coughlin addresses have been disproven. Evidence is produced in quantities to prove that he accepts hearsay, discredited writers, periodicals, and books, and even Nazi propaganda "handouts" as authentic sources for his information.

How, then, can Father Coughlin presume to call himself "scientific"? How can he presume to Transfer to his ideas the sanctity of the Roman Catholic Church? The only answers to these questions is that he—like all propagandists who care only for the attainment of their own immediate goals—presumes what he pleases. He is either merely careless with facts or incurious. "A lie," wrote Adolf Hitler in *Mein Kampf* (*My Struggle*), "is believed because of the unconditional and insolent inflexibility with which it is propagated and because it takes advantage of the sentimental and extreme sympathies of the masses. . . . Therefore, something always is retained even from the most impudent of lies." And lies, we must remember, take a vast number of forms, the chief seven of which are the *unfair* applications of our seven Propaganda Devices.

Testimonial consists in having some respected or hated person say that a given idea or program or product or person is good or bad.

VII. Testimonial

And now, ladies and gentlemen: We will hear from Chief Big Bear himself—*in person!*

Chief Big Bear will tell you how he discovered the "Million-Dollar Chief Big Bear Snake Oil" and how he discovered it *just in the nick of time* to save his *whole tribe* from dying of rheumatism, jaundice, Bright's disease, pneumonia, and many other horrible diseases and disorders and afflictions not known in this *civilized community*.

Chief Big Bear will speak to you in his own native Indian language. He will tell you about his *wonderful panacea* in his own words, and I—his long time friend and *adopted son*—will translate for you his words of wisdom. . . .

THIS is the classic misuse of the Testimonial Device that comes to the minds of most of us when we hear the term. We recall it indulgently and tell ourselves how much more sophisticated we are than our grandparents or even our parents.

With our next breath, we begin a sentence, "The *Times* said . . .," "John L. Lewis said . . .," "Herbert Hoover said . . .," "The President said . . .," "My doctor said . . .," or "Our minister said . . ." Some of these Testimonials may merely give greater emphasis to a legitimate and accurate idea, a fair use of the device;

others, however, may represent the sugar-coating of a distortion, a falsehood, a misunderstood notion, an anti-social suggestion. The rest of such sentences may, of course, have given the impression that "So-and-so, a bad man, advocates such-and-such an idea, and *therefore* the idea is bad," or that "So-and-so, a good man, advocates such-and-such an idea, and *therefore* the idea is good."

In short, *Testimonial is the fourth device used by skillful and dangerous propagandists to convince us of an idea before we become critical and examine the evidence in the case.* It is *also* the fourth device—in our list of seven—used by *fair* propagandists to interest us in a useful idea so that we will examine the evidence and may eventually accept the proposal.

To beat bad propagandists at their game *or* to prove to ourselves that the propagandas we like are really as good as they sound to us, we will all do well to ask ourselves the following questions regarding each Testimonial we hear:

Who or what is quoted in the Testimonial?

Why should we regard this person (or organization or publication or whatnot) as having expert knowledge or trustworthy information or reliable opinion on the subject in question?

Above all, what does the idea amount to on its own merits, without the benefit of the Testimonial?

Father Coughlin's Testimonials. Father Coughlin's speeches contain illustrations of three ways in which the Testimonial Device may be utilized unfairly. These three ways are:

1. The use of untrustworthy sources.
2. The distortion of facts or opinions contained in and attributed to trustworthy sources.

3. The alleged quotation of facts or opinions from a reputable source that do not come from that source.

Let us illustrate these devices with several examples.

In Father Coughlin's "defense mechanism" theory of Communism and Nazism, described in the chapters on Name Calling and Glittering Generality, he stresses the "fact" that Jewish bankers and particularly American Jewish bankers financed the Russian Communist revolution of 1917. To bolster up this allegation, he asserted on November 20:

> In our possession, we have a copy of the official White Paper ⚥ issued by the English war cabinet in 1919. This official paper ⚥ prints the names of the Jewish bankers, Kuhn, Loeb and Company of New York, among those who helped to finance the Russian Revolution and Communism. Since then both Jewish and Gentile financiers have been according financial comfort to the Soviet Republic. Perhaps this financial overture was made in innocence—perhaps not.

His accuracy was challenged on this alleged quotation (see way 3 above) from the White Paper entitled *A Collection of Reports on Bolshevism in Russia*, published by the British government in April, 1919. *Nowhere in the three editions of this document is the name of Kuhn, Loeb & Co. so much as mentioned.*

Thus confronted, Father Coughlin shifted on November 27 to a different source, a source that is branded as untrustworthy and anti-Jewish by Monsignor John A. Ryan, eminent Catholic historian of the Catholic University of America, Washington, D. C. Father Coughlin turned to a book written by Rev. Denis Fahey, Professor of Philosophy at Blackrock Seminary, Dublin, Ireland, entitled *The Mystical Body of Christ in the Modern*

World. He quoted from Father Fahey (see way 1 above) as follows:

The chief document treating of the financing of the Russian Revolution is the one drawn up by the American Secret Service ⚭ and transmitted by the French High Commissioner ⚭ to his Government. It was published by the *Documentation Catholique* of Paris ⚭ on March 6, 1920, and was preceded by the following remarks, namely: "The authenticity of this document is guaranteed to us. With regard to its exactness, the exactness of the information which it contains, the American Secret Service ⚭ takes a responsibility." Now, in Section One of this official report ⚭ we read: "It was found out that the following persons as well as the banking house mentioned were engaged in this work of destruction: Jacob Schiff; Guggenheim; Max Breitung; Kuhn, Loeb & Co., of which the following are the directors: Jacob Schiff, Felix Warburg, Otto Kahn, Mortimer Schiff, S. H. Hanauer—all Jews. There can be no doubt that the Russian Revolution, which broke out a year after the information given above had been received, was launched and fomented by distinctively Jewish influence."

What is *Documentation Catholique* of Paris? Who in our Secret Service "guaranteed" the "authenticity of this document"? These are questions members of Father Coughlin's radio audience could answer only with the greatest difficulty. The answer, however, appeared in an official statement released to the press for publication the next day, November 28, 1938, by Frank J. Wilson, Chief of the United States Secret Service. Newspapers throughout the land quoted Chief Wilson as follows:

We have had several inquiries by newspapermen about statements made by Father Coughlin in a radio address yesterday. Father Coughlin is reported to have read paragraphs which he said were taken from a book or article written by Denis Fahey, whom he described as a Professor of Philosophy at Blackrock Seminary, Dublin, Ireland. The extract attributed to Professor Fahey in turn purports to quote from a document published in 1920 by *Documentation Catholique* of Paris, which ascribes to "The American Secret Service" responsibility for statements said to have been furnished to the French High Commissioner dealing with the financing of the Russian revolution of 1917.

The only United States governmental agency having the name of "Secret Service" is the United States Secret Service, which is a division of the Treasury Department. I have investigated our records and questioned members of the service who were on duty from 1916 to 1920, including my predecessor, William H. Moran, with respect to the statements made and quoted by Father Coughlin. They know of no such investigation or report as that which Father Coughlin discussed, and it is quite certain that no such report was ever made by the United States Secret Service.

Chief Wilson's statement is adequate proof that Father Coughlin used in this, as in so many other instances, an untrustworthy source (Fahey's book) which in turn falsely quoted a reputable source (the United States Secret Service). In addition, the daily newspapers of November 28th printed a statement from Kuhn, Loeb & Co. that that firm "has never had any financial relations, or other relations, with any government in Russia, whether Czarist, Kerensky, or Communist," and that none of its partners, "past or present, assisted in any way to finance the Communist revolution in Russia or anywhere else."

The disproval of Father Coughlin's facts bring no retractions and no modifications of his theories. He merely shifts, without apology, to another allegedly trustworthy source, uses another Testimonial ⚖. When he was confronted with Wilson's and Kuhn, Loeb & Co.'s statements, he ascribed new powers to Fahey. This necessitated, of course, making Fahey somehow privileged to obtain confidential papers of the British government. Let us look at this shift in Father Coughlin's address of December 4th. He took up his new position thus:

Once more, then, I hereby refer to the British White Paper ✡ which contains documentary evidence received from the Secret Service ✡. The existence of this White Paper and of the reports incorporated therein cannot be brushed aside by idle denial.

Last week I telephoned to Dr. Denis Fahey ✡, Blackrock Seminary, Dublin, Ireland, asking him to re-inspect an original British White Paper ✡ from which I quoted. He assures me ✡ that an original copy ✡ is still available, safely guarded and at my disposal. And he assures me ✡ that it contains not only the references which I made to it last week, but also the excerpts from which I am about to read now in connection with the assertion by Kuhn, Loeb & Co. to the effect that neither the firm of Kuhn, Loeb & Co. nor any of its partners, past or present, assisted in any way to finance the Communist Revolution in Russia or anywhere else.

Section 8 of this British White Paper ✡ reads as follows: "If we bear in mind the fact that the Jewish banking house of Kuhn, Loeb & Co. is in touch with the Westphalian Rhineland Syndicate, German-Jewish house, and with the Brothers Lazard, Jewish house in Paris, and also with the Jewish house of Gunsberg of Petrograd, Tokio and Paris—if in addition we remark that all of the above-mentioned Jewish houses are in close correspondence with the Jewish house of Speyer & Co. of London, New York and Frankfort-on-the-Main, as well as with the Neibanken, Judeo-Bolshevik establishment in Stockholm, it will be manifest that the Bolshevist movement is in a certain measure the expression of a general Jewish movement and that certain Jewish banking houses are interested in the organization of this movement."

The telephone call to Dublin was a needless dressing up of Father Coughlin's Testimonial ⚭ distortion. The document to which he refers and from which he claims he obtained his quotations may be obtained in any large public or university library in the United States. The New York Public Library has available a copy of each of the three editions of this publication, entitled *A Collection of Reports on Bolshevism in Russia,* the only report to which Father Coughlin or Dr. Fahey could have legitimately referred. As we said earlier in this chapter, *nowhere in this document is the name of Kuhn, Loeb & Co. so much as mentioned.* In addition, *the document contains no reference to any "American" or "United States Secret Service" report.*

In the foregoing, we have shown how Father Coughlin has used the first three unfair applications of the Testimonial Device. Before going on to tell from whence his "facts" in this case probably came, let us consider an analysis of this sequence of Coughlin Testimonials made by Monsignor John A. Ryan. Monsignor Ryan investigated Coughlin's "evidence" thoroughly and published a report in *The Commonweal* of December 30, 1938, from which the following excerpts are taken:

Here then we have the ultimate alleged source of the list. Father Coughlin quotes Father Fahey, who quotes the *Patriot,* which quotes the *Documentation Catholique,* which declares that "the American Secret Service takes responsibility." Unfortunately for this "cloud of witnesses," Chief Wilson of the United States Secret Service declared, November 28, 1938, after an exhaustive search of the records and consultation of the members of the service on duty from 1916 to 1920: "It is quite certain that no such report was ever made by the United States Secret Service." Indeed, its phraseology suggests that it is anti-Semitic propaganda, rather than the report of an agency of the United States Government.

Where did Father Coughlin, then, get the information that he inaccurately attributes to the United States Secret Service and to the British White Paper? Did he make it up "out of the whole cloth"? No. The source, whether Father Coughlin's by direct quotation or by quotation of quotations in the *Documentation Catholique*, *The Patriot*, and Fahey's book, is the Nazi propaganda sheet, *World-Service*. *World-Service*, a leaflet circulated by the Nazis to "reveal" the "machinations of the Jewish under-world," published the information Father Coughlin gave in his address of December 4, 1938, in its issue of February 15, 1936. This document is reproduced on the following page so that readers may see how Father Coughlin *incorporated virtually the actual language* of the *World-Service* story into his speech.

But Father Coughlin did not depend wholly in his speech of December 4th upon this *World-Service* quotation that he alleged appeared in a British White Paper. He attempted to bolster up this Testimonial with another. He referred to "another collection of documents known as the Sisson Report." He did this as follows:

Let me elaborate by referring to another collection of documents known as the Sisson Report ⚘. This latter collection of documents, whose authenticity is guaranteed by the National Board for Historical Service of the United States ⚘ and is accepted by the United States Congress ⚘, is official. Document No. 57 of the Sisson Report is a circular issued on November 2, 1914. Among other things, it says: "Zinoviev and Lunacharsky got in touch with the Imperial Bank of Germany through the bankers, Rubenstein, Max Warburg, and Parvus. Zinoviev addressed himself to Rubenstein and Lunacharsky

The issue of the Nazi propaganda leaflet, *World-Service*, containing material that Father Coughlin *incorporated virtually word for word* into his speech of December 4, 1938.

through Altvater to Warburg, through whom he found support in Parvus." Here, then, the international bankers, among them a Warburg of the same family of Warburgs associated with the Kuhn, Loeb bank, is one of the internationalists aiding and abetting revolution. Document 64 of this same official government report ⚭ is a letter written by J. Furstenberg to Raphel Scholan on September 21, 1917, and it says: "Dear Comrade: The office of the banking house M. Warburg has opened in accordance with telegram from President of Rhenish-Westphalian Syndicate an account for the undertaking of Comrade Trotsky. . . . Signed J. Furstenberg."

In the first place, Father Coughlin made two errors on the very surface: The National Board for Historical Service, in existence in 1918, was not "of the United States" in the sense of being connected with the Federal Government; it was a private organization. No report of a private organization is accepted by the United States Congress as official.

The Sisson Report appeared in a booklet entitled *The German Bolshevik Conspiracy*, published in October, 1918, by the Federal Committee on Public Information, our World War Propaganda bureau of which George Creel was Chairman. This booklet contains documents that refer to German activity in aiding and fomenting the Bolshevik revolution in Russia. At Creel's request, a committee of the National Board for Historical Service—a private organization—examined the documents to determine their authenticity. This committee's report, printed in the Creel booklet with the documents, has this to say about Documents 57 and 64, the ones quoted by Father Coughlin:

III. For the documents of our third group, apart from Nos. 56 and 58, we have only the Russian mimeographed texts. The originals of nearly all of them would have been written in German. We have seen neither originals nor photographs, nor has Mr. Sisson, who rightly relegates these documents to an appendix, and expresses less confidence in their evidential value than in that of his main series, Nos. 1 to 53. With such insufficient means of testing their genuineness as can be afforded by Russian translations, we can make no confident declaration.

And Father Coughlin represents this as a guarantee of "authenticity"! It is precisely the opposite.

Not satisfied with a fictitious Secret Service report, with falsified quotations from a British White Paper, and with an extreme distortion of the Sisson Report, Father Coughlin also presented in his December 4th address this information:

> Now, supplementing all these documents ⚘ that I have quoted, . . . may I produce the startling evidence of another governmental document ⚘ as a refutation. It is a document published by the United States Department of State ⚘ in a now rare volume entitled, "Papers Relating to the Foreign Relations of the United States." 1917, Supplement 2, the World War, Volume I, Page 25, File No. 763, 72119, 5638 ⚘; it reads as follows: "The Secretary of State to the Ambassador in Russia, Mr. Francis, Washington, April 16, 1917, #1321. Please deliver following telegram. (I am only quoting the last two sentences.) We are confident Russian Jewry are ready for the greatest sacrifices in support of the present democratic government as the only hope for the future of Russia and all its people. American Jewry holds itself ready to co-operate with the Russian brethren in this great movement. Marshall, Morgenthau, Schiff, Straus, Rosenwald. Addressee Miliukov, Petrograd, or Baron Gunzburg. If sent to Baron Gunzburg add, 'May we ask you to submit this to your government.' Signed Lansing."

My friends, comment upon this startling document is almost unnecessary. Two names of the Kuhn, Loeb firm, Schiff and Straus, are mentioned in this telegram by the Secretary of the United States, Secretary of State Robert Lansing. What is more important and of astounding interest, my friends, you learn from this communication that Woodrow Wilson's Secretary of State, Robert Lansing, was in this instance and in his official capacity the secretary of the Jewish international bankers in helping to plot revolution with its subsequent mass murder and practical atheism.

Let us pass over the fact that Jacob H. Schiff is the only banker on the list and that Straus—Oscar Straus, perhaps—was not and never has been a member of Kuhn, Loeb & Co.

The *facts* of the case, to which Father Coughlin was apparently oblivious, are these: This cable was sent on April 16, 1917. Czar Nicholas had abdicated on March 15, 1917, in favor of a provisional government which the United States recognized on March 19th. This provisional government was democratic and was so acclaimed by the advocates of liberty and democracy throughout the world. Father Coughlin, however, heaped his contempt on this revolution as one "which for shortness of life and insignificance of effect will be classified with the frequent uprisings which come and go with every sunset in Central America." President Woodrow Wilson, on the contrary, expressed the sentiments of the American people in his war message of April 2, 1917, when he said that "the great, generous Russian people have been added in all their naive majesty and might to the forces that are fighting for freedom in the world, for justice, and for peace."

Russia had been, and, as a democratic nation, remained our ally. The only way in which messages might be transmitted to Russia was through diplomatic channels. The volume from which Father Coughlin quoted, not "rare" but easily available to anyone interested, contains many other such messages. Leaders of American Jewry were loyally pledging their support to "the present democratic government"—the *pre-Soviet* government—in Russia as a means of insuring an Allied victory. They were far from conspiring to establish the Soviet régime; the Imperial German government, as we have shown, conspired along that line. But Coughlin deleted a reference contained in the message to "the present democratic government."

Let us give one more example of Father Coughlin's unfair use of Testimonials. In an article in the December 5, 1938, issue of his magazine, *Social Justice,* he published an article under his signature entitled "Background of Persecution." It was soon discovered by Sam O'Neal of the St. Louis *Star-Times* Washington Bureau that this article contained strange parallelisms to a speech delivered by Paul Joseph Goebbels, Nazi Minister of Propaganda and Public Enlightenment, before the seventh National Socialist Party conference at Nuremberg on September 13, 1935. These parallelisms, as presented in the St. Louis *Star-Times* of December 31, 1938, are as follows:

GOEBBELS: "On April 30, 1919, in the courtyard of the Luitpold Gymnasium, in Munich, ten hostages, among them one woman, were shot through the backs, their bodies rendered unrecognizable and taken away. This act was done at the order of the Communist terrorist, Egelhofer, and under the responsibility of the Jewish Soviet commissars, Levien, Levine-Nissen and Axelrod."

FATHER COUGHLIN: "On April 30, 1919, in the courtyard of the Luitpold Gymnasium, in Munich, ten hostages, among them one woman, were murdered. This act was perpetrated by the direct order of the Communist terrorist, Egelhofer, and under the responsibility of the Jewish Soviet commissars, Levien, Levine-Nissen and Axelrod."

GOEBBELS: "The Jewish Tschekist, Bela Kun, made an experiment which rivaled the Paris Commune in bloodshed when he ordered the execution of 60,000 to 70,000 people in the Crimea. For the most part these executions were carried out with machine guns. At the Municipal Hospital in Alupka 272 sick and wounded were brought out on stretchers in front of the gate of the institution and there shot."

FATHER COUGHLIN: "At a later date, the same Bela Kun ordered the execution of approximately 60,000 people in the Crimea. For the most part these executions were carried out with machine guns. At the Municipal Hospital in Alupka, 272 sick and wounded were brought out on stretchers in front of the gate of the institution and there shot."

GOEBBELS: "November, 1934, the Chinese marshal, Chiang Kai-shek, made public the information that in the province of Kiangsi one million people were murdered by the Communists and six millions robbed of their possessions."

FATHER COUGHLIN: "In November, 1934, the Chinese marshal, Chiang Kai-shek, made public the information that in the province of Kiangsi one million people were murdered by the Communists and six million robbed of their possessions."

GOEBBELS: "The Soviet statistician, Oganowsky, estimates the number of persons who died of hunger in the years 1921, 1922, at 5,200,000."

FATHER COUGHLIN: "The Soviet statistician, Oganowsky, estimated the number of persons who died of hunger in the years 1921-1922 at more than 5,000,000."

GOEBBELS: "The Austrian Cardinal-Archbishop Monsignor Innitzer said in his appeal of July, 1934, that mil-

FATHER COUGHLIN: "The Austrian Cardinal-Archbishop, Monsignor Innitzer, said in his appeal of July, 1934, that

lions of people were dying of hunger throughout the Soviet Union."

GOEBBELS: "The most boorish example of the interference of 'Soviet diplomats' for the purpose of creating domestic political trouble in another country is afforded by the Jewish Soviet ambassador, Joffe, who had to leave Berlin on the 6th of November, 1918, because he had utilized the diplomatic courier to transport sabotage material which was to be used to undermine the German army and make the revolution possible."

GOEBBELS: "On the 26th December, 1918, one of the Socialist members of the Reichstag, the Jew, Dr. Oskar Cohn, declared that on the 5th of the previous month, he had received four million rubles from Joffe for the purpose of the German revolution.

"At the second Congress of Atheists, Bucharin declared that religion must be 'destroyed with the bayonet.'"

millions of people were dying of hunger throughout the Soviet Union."

FATHER COUGHLIN: "Before the advent of Hitler to power, Germany was undermined steadily by espionage of the most treasonable kind. The Jewish Soviet ambassador, Joffe, was forced to leave Germany on November 6, 1918, because he was found guilty of utilizing the diplomatic courier to transport sabotage material which was used to undermine the German army and make revolution possible."

FATHER COUGHLIN: "On the 26th of December, 1918, one of the Socialist members of the Reichstag, the eminent Jew, Dr. Oskar Cohn, declared that on the 5th of the previous month he had received four million rubles from Joffe for the purpose of instigating a revolution in Germany.

"Remember that, when the second Congress of Atheists convened, Bucharin declared that religion must be 'destroyed with the bayonet.'"

GOEBBELS: "The Social Democratic 'League of German Free Thinkers' alone had a membership of 600,000. The Communist 'League of Proletarian Free Thinkers' had close on 160,000 members. Almost without exception, the intellectual leaders of Marxist atheism in Germany were Jews, among them being Erich Weinert, Felix Abraham, Dr. Levy-Lenz and others. At regular meetings held in the presence of a notary public, members were requested to register their declaration of withdrawal from their church for a fee of two marks. And thus the fight for atheism was carried on. Between 1918 and 1933 the withdrawals from the German Evangelical churches alone amounted to two and a half million persons in Germany."

FATHER COUGHLIN: "In Germany the Social Democratic 'League of German Free Thinkers' had a membership of 600,000. The Communist 'League of Proletarian Free Thinkers' numbered close to 160,000 members. Almost without exception, the intellectual leaders— if not the foot and hand leaders—of Marxist atheism in Germany were Jews. Not good Jews but bad Jews; not Jews who opposed Communism but Jews who supported it. Among them were Erich Weinert, Felix Abraham and Dr. Levy-Lenz. At regular meetings held in the presence of a notary public, members were requested to register their declaration of withdrawal from their church for a fee of two marks. With such bribes the fight for atheism was carried on. And between 1918 and 1933 the withdrawals from the German Evangelical churches was estimated at close to two and a half million persons in Germany."

GOEBBELS: "In 1919, during the Bolshevic regime of

FATHER COUGHLIN: "In 1919 Hungary, a neighbor to

the Jew, Bela Kun, whose real name was Aron Cohn, in Budapest twenty hostages were murdered."

Germany, was overrun with Communists. The notorious atheist, Bela Kun, a Jew, whose real name was Aaron Cohn, murdered twenty hostages."

GOEBBELS: "The truth of this report has been officially confirmed by the Geneva Red Cross."

FATHER COUGHLIN: "The truth of this has been officially confirmed in the report made to the Geneva Red Cross."

GOEBBELS: "The Jew, Gubermann, who, under the name of Jaroslawski, is the leader of the Association of Militant Atheists in the Soviet Union, has made the following declaration:
"It is our duty to destroy every religious world concept. . . . If the destruction of ten million human beings, as happened in the last war, should be necessary for the triumph of one definite class, then that must be done and it will be done."

FATHER COUGHLIN: "The atheist Jew, Gubermann, under the name of Jaroslawski, and then the leader of the Militant Atheists in the Soviet Union also declared:
"It is our duty to destroy every religious world concept. . . . If the destruction of ten million human beings, as happened in the last war, should be necessary for the triumph of one definite class, then that must be done and it will be done."

In a telephone interview with O'Neal, Father Coughlin said, "It is unfortunate if there is any similarity between what I have written and what Goebbels has said." He attributed his quotations to material published some years ago by the Hungarian government and supplied to him by "Communicato Documento Catholique," a documentary service he said was conducted under the auspices of the Catholic Church in Paris.

When O'Neal asked Father Coughlin if his material might engender race hatreds in this country, the priest is quoted as replying:

No, no, no. I was not talking of any racial group. I don't think it any more a bad influence than if I used just a little effort to stir up Communist opposition as I'm going to do in a radio address next Sunday. . . .

I've become accustomed to unfair attacks in thirteen years. My shins are impervious to a few kicks.

The "coincidence," nevertheless, remains. The similarity of quotations at least shows that Father Coughlin and Goebbels respect the same sources for their "facts." But, as *Social Justice*, Father Coughlin's magazine, asserted on November 14, 1938:

THE ONLY SOURCE OF TRUTH IS FATHER COUGHLIN

A man who permits his mouthpiece to utter such a thing as that—a position even the Pope does not take in the Roman Catholic Church—may dare much.

VIII. Plain Folks

I glory in the fact that I am a simple Catholic priest endeavoring to inject Christianity into the fabric of an economic system woven upon the loom of greed by the cunning fingers of those who manipulate the shuttles of human lives for their own selfish purposes.

THIS is about as far as Father Coughlin cares to go in using the Plain Folks Device. Since he was not a house painter like Adolf Hitler or a corporal like Napoleon Bonaparte, he capitalizes upon the joint use of the Transfer Device and the Plain Folks Device by calling himself "a simple Catholic priest."

Rather than one of the Plain Folks, Father Coughlin tries to stand before his radio audience as one who is being persecuted for their sake, for the sake of "Americanism," for the sake of "democracy," for the sake of "Christ" and "Christianity," defining the meaning and spirit of these words to suit himself. A typical refrain is the one he used on January 15th, "Oh, they have persecuted me, and they will persecute you."

The Plain Folks Device was a strong weapon in the hands of Huey Long, and it serves well many another

Democratic and Republican politician both for socially desirable and undesirable purposes.

Father Coughlin's radio announcer, in "passing the hat" to pay the costs of the program and of Father Coughlin's other propagandistic efforts, is permitted to use the Plain Folks Device more directly. Before introducing Father Coughlin, he always says words to this effect:

> As you know, this hour is in no sense a donated hour. It is paid for at full commercial rates. This is your ℔ hour. This is your ℔ presentation. As long as you ℔ desire to have Father Coughlin a guest ℔ in your home ℔ each Sunday afternoon over these same stations, and at this same hour, he will be glad to speak fearlessly and courageously to you ℔, as he presents a message of Christianity and Americanism to Catholics and Protestants and Religious Jews.

Since the Plain Folks pay for his broadcasts, we are all supposed to jump on the Band Wagon (see Chapter X) and send in our money.

Since Plain Folks is so widely used by other propagandists, however, it is well to discuss the device briefly here in a little more detail:

Politicians, labor leaders, business men, and even ministers and educators win our confidence by appearing to be people like ourselves—"just plain folks among the neighbors." In election years especially do candidates show their devotion to little children and the common, homey things of life. They have front porch campaigns. For the benefit of newspapermen, they raid the kitchen cupboard and find there some of the good wife's apple pie. They go to country picnics; they attend service at the old frame church; they pitch hay and go fishing; they show their belief in home and mother.

In short, these men would win our votes, business, or other support by showing that they're just as common as the rest of us—"salt of the earth"—and, therefore, wise and good.

Our defense against this device, when used by the undemocratic or the otherwise anti-social, is simply this: We must ask ourselves what the propagandist's ideas are worth when divorced from his personality. In other words:

What is he trying to cover up with his Plain Folks manner?

What are the facts?

Suspend judgment until we get enough evidence.

Card Stacking involves the selection and use of facts or falsehoods, illustrations or distractions, and logical or illogical statements in order to give the best or the worst possible case for an idea, program, person or product.

IX. Card Stacking

WHAT might well be called "monopolistic" Card Stacking is a direct violation of America's Cracker Barrel Philosophy. Around our traditional cracker barrels, we expect each of our local spokesmen to present his case—to stack the cards—for a given proposal in the best way that he can. But we also insist that other spokesmen *around the same cracker barrel* speak right up and stack the cards in favor of their alternative proposals. From these conflicting arrangements and interpretations of evidence, we know that some fairly sensible compromise is likely to come.

The dangers of "monopolistic" Card Stacking, of submitting ourselves to a barrage of evidence presented from but one viewpoint, are what prompted an editorial writer for the New York *Times* to observe on September 1, 1937: "What is truly vicious is not propaganda but a monopoly of it."

Americans do not object to Card Stacking, so long as the amenities of the cracker barrel are practiced, so long as we can at least demand of a speaker, "Yeah, but what about . . . ?" and get a reasonable answer. This accounts for the great enthusiasm with which such radio programs as "America's Town Meeting of the Air" and "The University of Chicago Round Table" are received.

But all speakers, even in the United States, apparently do not feel that they can present the cases for their proposals in competition with the cases for the proposals of others. Father Coughlin, for example, refused to take part in "America's Town Meeting of the Air" on January 19, 1939; he refused to participate in a discussion at the Columbia University Institute of Arts and Sciences, March, 1939, and in a discussion meeting of the Progressive Education Association at its convention in Detroit, February 25, 1939. Does Father Coughlin want to avoid an audience and competing speakers that will ask questions and expect to have them answered? Is it that he does not want to run the risk of having his undemocratic theories and methods exposed?

Even in declining the invitation to *discuss*—not debate— "What is Americanism?" at the January 19th "Town Meeting," Father Coughlin tried to stack the cards as well as to use other devices in his own favor. He asserted:

> Americanism is not a debatable subject with me nor is it controversial. . . . I am constrained to refuse your kind offer lest I be suspected 💬 of accepting a sop from the NBC 💬 and its censorial commissars.

Father Coughlin did not care to admit that the nationwide broadcasting networks follow enlightened Roman Catholic opinion in making their time available for programs that the Roman Catholic Church regards as more representative of its viewpoint. Except for political talks at election times, all religious and political programs are carried free and only on a free or "sustaining" basis by the major networks. No political or religious program may be presented, except at election times, in "paid time." *Representative* Protestant, Catholic, and Jewish organizations are allotted time on the networks free without prejudice. If Father Coughlin's "educational talks on economics and politics" were endorsed as representative of Roman Catholic views, he would still be given network radio time without cost.

The best proof that Father Coughlin, though a priest, does not represent Roman Catholic views is the statement issued by George Cardinal Mundelein of Chicago on December 11, 1938, mentioned elsewhere, that "he is not authorized to speak for the Catholic Church, nor does he represent the doctrine or sentiments of the Church."

When we are confronted with an effort at Card Stacking, such as the one mentioned and analyzed above, we must remind ourselves to suspend judgment on the propagandist's proposals until we have answered such questions as these:

Just what is the propagandist trying to "sell" us?

Is this proposal in line with our own best interests and the best interests of society, as we see them?

What are the alternative proposals?

What is the evidence for and against these alternatives?

Let us now illustrate the Card Stacking Device as it has been used in three instances by Father Coughlin. These instances are:

1. The "defense mechanism" theory of the rise of Communism and Nazism.

2. The confusion, in his discussions, of events connected with the Russian *democratic* revolution of 1917 with events associated with the Russian Soviet or Communist revolution of 1917, two different revolutions.

3. The Bridgeport and Cleveland cases of the "promotion of atheism" by Jewish organizations.

The first two are to be taken up together, and the last alone.

1 and 2: In the chapter on the Testimonial Device ⚏, evidence was produced to indicate the distortions upon which Father Coughlin based his charge that Jewish and Gentile international bankers inspired either the Russian *democratic* revolution of 1917 or the Russian Soviet or Communist revolution which followed so closely upon it. Evidence was also presented in the chapter on the Glittering Generality Device to demonstrate the anti-democratic propaganda involved in calling Nazism a "defense mechanism" against Communism or Communism a "defense mechanism" against the "greed of the money changers." These discussions, with their supporting facts, need not be repeated here. It is our purpose here merely to focus attention on this theory again as a prime example of Father Coughlin's unfair use of the Card Stacking Device and to correlate the strands of our analysis by presenting some additional materials bearing upon the theory.

The March, 1917, revolution in Russia was hailed throughout the democratic countries of the world and especially in the United States as a great victory both for the Allied cause and for democracy. President Woodrow Wilson, Elihu Root, Charles Evans Hughes, Joseph H. Choate, and ex-Presidents William Howard Taft and Theodore Roosevelt all joined in welcoming the new democracy. The Roman Catholic view of this victory of democracy over Czarism is indicated by a dispatch in the New York *Times* of March 23, 1917. Dated at Rome, it reports that the Vatican "at first was undecided what attitude to take in regard to the events in Russia but is gradually realizing that the new order of things is most advantageous from the Roman Catholic point of view." In addition, in July, 1917, religious leaders of all faiths, including Cardinal Gibbons of the Roman Catholic Church, signed their names to a call for "a universal intercession on the part of religious America on their behalf to Almighty God, to the end that the great convulsion in Russia may result in some form of governmental authority which shall assure to the people of that vast empire an orderly and enduring guarantee of peace and happiness, truth and justice, religion and piety."

Jacob H. Schiff, a leading American Jew and a member of Kuhn, Loeb & Co., added his voice to these many others in a telegram dated March 24, 1917, a few weeks before the United States entered the World War. This telegram, which Father Coughlin has quoted, is as follows:

Will you say for me to those present at tonight's meeting how deeply I regret my inability to celebrate with the friends of Russian freedom the actual reward of what we have hoped and striven for these long years.

Despite the fact that Alexander Kerensky, Premier of the Russian democratic government in 1917, is quoted in the New York *Times* of November 30, 1938, as saying, "the revolutionary government obtained credit not through any bankers, Jewish or Gentile in America, but from the United States Government," Father Coughlin replied, "I say that according to reputable testimony it was financed by Jacob Schiff."

We need not go far afield to refute this use of the Testimonial Device to stack cards in favor of Father Coughlin's theory. A United States Treasury report issued in 1927, entitled *Combined Annual Reports of the World War*

Foreign Debt Commission, lists the cash advances made by the United States government to Russia during the so-called Kerensky or democratic régime. These advances totaled $192,729,750.

Another aspect of Father Coughlin's "defense mechanism" theory also needs a little additional attention. He portrays Nazism not only as a "defense mechanism" against the Communism "inspired by atheistic Jews and Gentiles" in Russia but also as a "defense mechanism" against the Communism "inspired by atheistic Jews and Gentiles" in Germany. The part that Jews played in the Communist movement in Germany is well indicated by the election returns for the last free election before Hitler came into power, that of November, 1932. With not more than 300,000 of the 550,000 German Jews eligible to vote, there were 5,980,240 Communist votes cast. In other words, if *every* German Jewish voter had been a Communist, the German Jewish votes would have accounted for not more than five per cent of the total Communist vote. *Kuerschners Volkshandbuch Deutscher Reichstag* (*Kuerschner's Popular Handbook of the German Reichstag*) for 1933 indicates that *but one* of the 70 Communist deputies in the Reichstag of 1930 was Jewish. The leaders of Communism in Germany—Thaelmann and Torgler—were also both Gentiles.

This conclusive evidence does not keep Hitler from "taking advantage of the sentimental and extreme sympathies of the masses" to repeat his claim that he rescued Germany from "Jewish Communism." And Father Coughlin is apparently willing to rely for his facts and many of his interpretations upon such Nazi propaganda, regardless of his proclaimed opposition to both Nazism and Fascism.

Let us turn to other cases that illustrate other applications of Card Stacking in Father Coughlin's addresses:

3. *The Bridgeport and Cleveland cases of the "promotion of atheism" by Jewish organizations:* This Coughlin Card Stacking hinged on these statements:

In publishing the report of achievements accomplished by the Jewish Community Councils, we read on page 365 of the *B'nai B'rith National Jewish Monthly* for June, 1938, the following astounding admission ⟦•⟧:

"In Bridgeport and Cleveland, the councils persuaded public school officials to stop Easter and Christmas practices which had been embarrassing to the Jewish children and had found serious objection among Jewish parents who had hesitated to deal with the matter individually."

In referring to this remarkable quotation ⟦•⟧, the words I wish to emphasize are these: "Christmas and Easter practices." By "practices," I understand neither the teaching of religion, the reading and interpretation of the Bible, nor the common recitation of prayers ⟦•⟧. These words, "Christmas and Easter practices," connote for me the celebration of these two holidays—the interchanging of gifts; the singing of carols, associated with the crib and the empty tomb; and in submitting this quotation, I do not wish to infer that the Jewish Community Councils are totally responsible for eliminating Christ or religion from our schools ⟦•⟧.

Before we continue to quote from Father Coughlin's address of December 11, 1938, let us analyze his case so far. Since he devoted the equivalent of twelve typewritten pages to an elaboration of this idea, he apparently regarded it as far more significant than did the American Jewish Councils who gave the incident ten short lines in a lengthy report.

What did the Bridgeport and Cleveland Jewish Councils seek to accomplish? Within their members' rights as American citizens, guaranteed religious freedom by the Federal Constitution, these Councils merely wished to exempt Jewish children from taking part in ceremonies contrary to their faith. The school officials had no right to expect these children to sing carols or take part in pageants in which their parents had no faith. If public schools were using Catholic ritual it is quite likely that both Protestants and Jews would ask to have their children exempted; if Jewish ritual were used Protestants and Catholics probably would ask exemption for their children.

In other words, in this case as in the case described in the Glittering Generality chapter, Father Coughlin tries to stir up opposition to our Constitutional guarantee that "Congress shall make no law respecting an establishment of religion, or prohibiting the free exercise thereof," a guarantee made equally binding upon our minor governmental bodies by the fourteenth amendment.

Father Coughlin admits that he makes such an unconstitutional demand. He admits that he wishes a suspension of the religious freedom guarantee of the Federal Constitution. He at least wants the Jews to deny themselves this fundamental democratic right. As Father Coughlin puts his case:

I am glad to admit ⟨•⟩ that this organization is within its Constitutional rights. More than that, I admit that this action cannot by any stretch of the imagination be construed as intolerant ⟨•⟩. But I am not so illogical as to charge that the Jews alone ⟨•⟩ have been responsible for banishing religion from our educational institutions ⟨•⟩. Many influences and policies originating from non-Jewish quarters have contributed their major share towards this unhappy condition ⟨•⟩. I am not so illogical as to charge that organized Jewry in America is opposed to the preachments and practices of Christianity within the walls of our Churches or under the roofs of our homes ⊡. But I am logical enough to comprehend and appreciate ⊡ the truthfulness of Lenin's statement: "Give me a child for three years, and I will hand you back a Communist." And I am Christian enough to assert that if God will remain expatriated ⊡ from our schools, these public institutions will begin to contribute towards graduating a Godless generation. . . .

Intolerance towards men is always reprehensible. But oftentimes, intolerance is provoked by injudicious and erroneous policies ⊡. Therefore, I appeal to the General Jewish Councils, and the local Councils—I ask you, even if you are within your Constitutional rights, even though we dare not ⊡ protest legally—why have you closed the minds of our children Constitutionally to the beautiful story of Bethlehem and the Messias (Messiah) ⊡? Was not that an act of poor judgment? Why have you blotted out ⊡ the cycle of the Easter story, its crucifixion and its glorious resurrection of the victim of mob violence and hate?

To a believer in democracy, these statements represent a series of *nonsequiturs*, of illogically related ideas. The insidiousness of this propaganda, despite its logical absurdity, is well revealed by answering some of Father Coughlin's rhetorical questions:

"Why have you closed the minds of our children Constitutionally to the beautiful story of Bethlehem and the Messias (Messiah)?" The only fair answer to this unfairly put question is that the various Jewish Councils have not "closed the minds" of any non-Jews to any aspect of Christianity. Certainly the Roman Catholic Church has never depended upon religious teachings in public schools to assure the fidelity of Catholic children. Our laws permit the Catholics to have their own schools in which they may indoctrinate their own children as much as they see fit.

Democracy, let us repeat, regards religion as a *personal* and *not* a *political or national* problem.

"Was not that an act of poor judgment?" Father Coughlin asked next. This question assumes that the immediately preceding question must be answered affirmatively, that Jews have "closed the minds of our children Constitutionally to the beautiful story of Bethlehem and the Messias (Messiah)." In other words, under the guise of open-minded questioning, Father Coughlin makes dogmatic statements of what he later assumes to be fact.

When one views these statements in cold type and analytically, they become far less convincing—they more readily reveal his "game"—than when they come thundering over the radio. In type, it is all too apparent that even in excusing Jews from "intolerance" Father Coughlin's statements suggest that he is really being "too tolerant" of "Jewish intolerance"! In addition, he says he is "not so illogical as to charge that organized Jewry in America is opposed to the preachments and practices of Christianity within the walls of our Churches or under the roofs of our homes," and then he immediately injects a quotation from Lenin—rather than a popular and very similar one by Cardinal Newman—in order to suggest by inference that the public schools and the Jews are promoting Communism by the way of "atheism." The Lenin reference and quotation were injected all too obviously for the purpose of suggesting that Jews see eye to eye with Lenin in their political views, a suggestion in radical opposition to the facts, as we have shown elsewhere. For a Roman Catholic priest to attack the public school system directly would, as Father Coughlin well knows, be quite impolitic. But his equally unfair indirect methods are all too safe from correct interpretation through hasty analysis.

Band Wagon has as its theme, "Everybody—at least all of *us*—is doing it"; with it, the propagandist attempts to convince us that all members of a group to which we belong are accepting his program and that we must therefore follow our crowd and "jump on the band wagon."

X. Band Wagon

THE BAND WAGON is a means for making us follow the crowd and accept a propagandist's program as a whole and without examining the evidence for and against it. His theme is: "Everybody's doing it. Why not you?" His techniques range from those of the street-corner medicine show to those of the vast pageant.

The propagandist hires a hall, rents radio stations, fills a great stadium, marches a million or at least a lot of men in a parade. He employs symbols, colors, music, movement, all the dramatic arts. He gets us to write letters, to send telegrams, to contribute to his "cause." He appeals to the desire, common to most of us, to "follow the crowd." Because he wants us to follow the crowd in masses, he directs his appeal to groups held together already by common ties, ties of nationality, religion, race, sex, vocation. Thus propagandists campaigning for or against a program will appeal to us as Catholics, Protestants, or Jews; as members of the Nordic race or as Negroes; as farmers or as school teachers; as housewives or as miners.

With the aid of all the other Propaganda Devices, all of the artifices of flattery are used to harness the fears and hatreds, prejudices and biases, convictions and ideals common to a group. Thus is emotion made to push and pull us as members of a group onto a Band Wagon.

"Don't throw away your vote. Vote for our candidate. He's winning." Nearly every candidate wins in every election *before the votes are in and counted.*

What can *we* do about the Band Wagon? Here are the questions we should certainly ask ourselves and should answer before we succumb to its wiles:

What is this propagandist's program?

What is the evidence for and against his program?

Does his program serve or undermine the interests of the group—my group—that he says favors him and his ideas?

No fair use of the Band Wagon Device can suffer from such questioning. And there is never as much of a rush to climb onto the Band Wagon as the propagandist tries to make us think there is.

Father Coughlin's Band Wagon Tactics. Father Coughlin makes repeated use of this device. He constantly attempts to stir up our emotions through appealing to us as Americans faced with national catastrophe, as believers in democracy faced with the downfall of this treasured political philosophy, and as Christians faced with the threat of spreading atheism. And then, assuming the existence of such a threat, he goes on to give us *the* way—*his* way—of avoiding the impending misfortune, not only *his* way but usually a way that involves the surrender of some cherished principle of Americanism, democracy, or even Christianity.

Let us take one example of Father Coughlin's use of

this device from the many available. The following, from his address of January 1, 1939, will serve to illustrate:

1939 finds Americans ☞ standing at the barricade of liberty. Behind us ☞ stretch 162 years of freedom, and before us ☞ yawns the vortex of national doom; behind us ☞ five generations of civic and industrial growth, before us ☞ beckons the specter of commercial decay and industrial slavery. Behind us ☞ stands gaunt and threatening the ogre of irreligion, of hate, and of war.

After thus appealing to us to stand forth against dangers stated in omnibus words, Father Coughlin went on to tell his "fellow citizens" that the "future of America" depends upon the answer to this question:

Shall we ☞ participate in an European war and degenerate into dictatorship, or shall we ☞ organize to preserve democracy, our Constitution, and keep clear of foreign entanglements?

Under this appeal to us as Americans with a noble tradition, under this barrage of oratory, Father Coughlin is trying to enlist us in a crusade to help the Spanish Rebels led by General Francisco Franco. To accomplish this purpose, Father Coughlin attempts to undermine our reverence for the President of the United States and for our Federal Government by alleging a conspiracy for the President to set up a dictatorship under a proposed law (the May bill that would give the President in the case of war powers similar to those exercised by President Wilson during the World War). In Father Coughlin's speeches of January 1, 8, and 15, he then attempts to "prove" that a lifting of the arms embargo against Loyalist Spain would be a step towards entering us in a war and hence a step towards placing the (proposed) "dictator-ship law" in effect.

The merits of the "May bill" are incidental to this prop-aganda theory. Father Coughlin's purpose is to stop the "spread of atheism" through hampering the efforts of the Spanish Loyalist government to put down the armed re-bellion against it led by General Franco. He calls the Loy-alist government "atheistic" because it has some backing from the Soviet Union. But, it is significant to note, he does not call General Franco a Nazi or Fascist even though General Franco has been aided by both the Ger-man and the Italian governments and has been openly using regiments of Italian troops in his campaigns.

The facts that will reveal the merits of both the "May bill" and the proposed lifting of the Spanish embargo are rendered even more obscure by Father Coughlin's argu-ments. Rather than permit ourselves in such cases to be stampeded into a position, therefore, it is a lot safer to take the advice so often repeated in this book: *Suspend judg-ment until the evidence is more apparent and satisfying.* Do not overlook the seven ABC's of Propaganda Analysis. And above all, do not permit any of the seven Propaganda Devices to take the place in your thinking of a candid sur-vey of the evidence.

XI. The Tricks in Operation

IN THE preceding chapters, each of the tricks of the propagandist's trade has been illustrated separately with materials drawn from recent radio orations by Father Coughlin. Let's take a whole speech now and show all these tricks in operation and relation with one another.

Father Coughlin's address of February 26, 1939, is selected for our purpose because in that address, probably more than in any other, the similarities between Father Coughlin's propaganda techniques and those of Adolf Hitler can readily be seen. This is true not only because of its distortions of fact and its unfair use of the seven Propaganda Devices, but also because the economic program that Father Coughlin outlines in the address so closely parallels the economic program of the Nazi Party before it rose to power. Of the latter, the May, 1938, issue of *Propaganda Analysis*, "The Propaganda Techniques of German Fascism," has said:

Then came Adolf Hitler, a leader, who promised the people all that they wanted. Most Germans felt that conditions were too bad even to question how all that he offered could be achieved. The few who did raise their voices in protest or doubt were silenced by argument, by force, or by honest conviction that this new scheme, this new hope, must be tried. Everything was promised to everyone; socialism to the laborer and to the more liberal Kleinburger; partition of the great estates to the peasant; dissolution of the trusts and economic security to the middle class citizen; salvation from communism to the upper bourgeois; and to everyone elimination of the Jews, rearmament of the Reich, and "national liberation."

"Everything was promised to everyone." That was Adolf Hitler's tactic. And that, as will be seen, is also Father Coughlin's.

Similarly, Father Coughlin employs the Nazi technique of praising democracy when it suits his purpose, of denouncing it vehemently on every other occasion. Thus, in this address of February 26, 1939, he expresses solicitude over the future of democracy, offering his program as the only way of saving it from its enemies. Yet, on August 1, 1938, Father Coughlin's magazine, *Social Justice*, said:

Democracy! More honored in the breach than in the observance.

Democracy! A mockery that mouths the word and obstructs every effort on the part of an honest people to establish a government for the welfare of the people.

Democracy! A cloak under which hide the culprits who have built up an inorganic tumor of government which is sapping away the wealth of its citizens through confiscatory taxation.

In like vein did Father Coughlin speak on November 6, 1938. Discussing the French Revolution, he declaimed contemptuously on the manner in which democracies glorify "the magic of numbers." He said that "a new king was set upon the throne of Notre Dame in Paris—the king symbolizing the magic of numbers, the king which said, 'mankind is king and the majority opinion shall prevail.' " This "magic of numbers"—democracy—he blamed for having "religiously kept religion out of government and fanatically denied the entrance of Christ's principles into economy, business, industry and agriculture." Father

Coughlin refuses to understand that democracy, as our democratic leaders have made abundantly clear many times, is a practical political philosophy based upon Christ's advocacy of the brotherhood of man.

One might well ask how anybody who has spoken of democracy so can later presume to pose as its defender. However, as the January, 1939, issue of *Propaganda Analysis*, "The Attack on Democracy," said:

At other times, when it suits their purpose, the American fascists can become quite tender in their attitude toward democracy, and charge that "World Jewry" is seeking to undermine it. This was their cry during the Supreme Court fight. More often, they praise democracy and fascism at one and the same time: in fact, they insist that America must go fascist if our democratic institutions are to endure. Thus, Robert Edmondson urges press dictatorship to achieve "freedom of the press." The American Nationalist Confederation demands "A Fascist Union for the Americas" in order to maintain American principles and "our republican form of government." *Deutscher Weckruf und Beobachter—The Free American*, official publication of the German-American Bund and the German-American Business League, Inc., denies that Adolf Hitler is dictator of Germany, insisting that Germany today is far more democratic than it has ever been.

Often, in the very same issue, *The Free American* will sing the praises of democracy in one article, only to assail democracy in the next.

All this may sound fantastic. And it may be wondered how anyone could hope to gain popular support, who contradicted himself so openly and so frequently. The demagogue knows, however, that few will bother to analyze what he says, and through analysis to expose the contradictions. "Most Germans felt that conditions were too bad even to question how all that he (Adolf Hitler) offered could be achieved." Not questioning, not analyzing, they followed blindly—to Nazi dictatorship.

With this background let us view a Coughlin "educational talk on politics and economics" as a whole. Let us take his speech of February 26, 1939, and see Father Coughlin's tricks in operation:

Good afternoon, my friends �. Last Monday evening, Madison Square Garden, New York City, was the scene of a Nazi Bund rally. Although the Acting Mayor of the City appealed to the citizens to remain away from the vicinity of the Garden, nearly one hundred thousand persons jostled about outside the building, and twenty-two thousand gained admission �.[1] The advertised occasion was a George Washington birthday celebration. The swastika and the Stars and Stripes were proudly � displayed on the platform, which was well guarded � by hundreds of uniformed Nazis of German, Italian, Irish and Polish extraction �.[2]

Absent from the meeting was the spirit of ideal � [3]

[1] Father Coughlin here is being rather vague. Does he mean to imply that approximately 120,000 New Yorkers sought to attend the celebration, but that only 22,000 could gain admission? Moreover, the figure of 22,000 admissions was the one announced by leaders of the Bund. The official police figure was 19,000.

[2] The Washington Day celebration of the German-American Bund was as perfect an example of the Transfer Device as could be imagined. Through it, the Nazis attempted to gain for their movement some of the reverence in which George Washington is held by the American people. They sought to gain for the swastika the prestige and sanctity of the Stars and Stripes.

Incidentally, the Bund is for people of German birth or descent only, as witness its full name, "the German-American Bund." Is Father Coughlin seeking to create the impression that Adolf Hitler's following in the United States is more widespread than would be imagined from the sponsorship of the Garden rally?

[3] Father Coughlin's technique in discussing Nazism is first to assail it, then gradually to soften his denunciation until it becomes praise.

Americanism ▨, which evidently obeyed the Acting Mayor's advice and remained at home. The next day, practically every newspaper in the nation reported the incident with front-page publicity, because it was a predominantly pro-Nazi ▣ [4] gathering. Nevertheless, thanks to the efficiency of New York's Police Department, no great disorder eventuated, either inside or outside the hall ▣.[5]

Considering all circumstances, no sane American ▨ rejoices [6] in such meetings as this Bund rally. Bear in mind that the occasion logically called for a demonstration of loyal Americanism ▨, but, paradoxically, the birthday of the Father of Our Country was seized not only to challenge Americans' opposition to Communism ▣,[7] but to publicize that this challenge originated from a pro-Nazi source ▣. Likewise paradoxical ▨ was a concurrent meeting held at Paris, France, the same day, and for the same advertised purpose ▨.[8]

Here we see how this is done. Instead of calling it "unAmerican" as others have, Father Coughlin speaks of Nazism as not being "ideal" Americanism.

[4] Father Coughlin is now going one step further in softening his denunciation. In the first paragraph, he called the meeting "Nazi." It now becomes "predominantly pro-Nazi."

[5] As every newspaper reader knows, there *was* disorder, leading Mayor LaGuardia to issue an order forbidding private armed guards at public meetings like the "hundreds of uniformed Nazis," to whom Father Coughlin referred in his opening paragraph.

[6] A mild word, indeed, to use in describing the reaction of the overwhelming majority of Americans to the Garden rally.

[7] As Father Coughlin well knows, the attacks on the Garden rally were *attacks on Nazism*. They were not made *to defend Communism*. We have examined several hundred newspaper editorials denouncing the rally. Not one "challenged Americans' opposition to Communism." To imply, as Father Coughlin does, that anyone who attacks Nazism is thereby defending Communism, is deliberately to disregard the fact that Americans overwhelmingly are opposed to *both* Communism and Nazism.

[8] Here the Transfer Device is being used in reverse: by lumping the Bund rally and the Paris meeting together, Father Coughlin seeks to transfer to the latter some of the unpopularity of the former.

Among the prominent speakers at Paris was Ambassador William Bullitt, who said that the United States was preoccupied with a growing apprehension that, if there should be a war in Europe, we might be drawn into it.

No official gave words, however, to Washington's thought on that 🔲 subject, a thought which expressed the principle of no foreign entanglements ⚱. These paradoxes 🐦 are symptomatic 🔲 of the trend of the times. They call for keen consideration, lest paradoxy 🐦 become orthodoxy in the immediate years to follow.

It is unfortunate 🐦 that such incidents must occur. They are merely the effects of certain causes. For the past ten years, Communists have been holding meetings in public places. On previous occasions, and to the dismay of millions, they filled Madison Square Garden and unfurled the red flag of Moscow. For years, the Communists have been busy boycotting German and Italian firms. Recently, these same well-organized Communists practiced disparagement against American citizens of German and Italian descent 🔲. Calmly considering 🌾 all these causes 🔲, they were bound 🔲 [9] to generate 🔲 the effect 🔲 of last Monday night. Unfortunately 🐦, this first Bund rally is only the beginning of a long series of incidents, unless the causes motivating them will be removed immediately.

Meanwhile, the vast majority of American citizens are still Americans 🌾. They are sympathetic neither with the Nazi Bund nor with the Communist contentions. They regard both

[9] Father Coughlin's theory is that "Communism generates Nazism," because "Nazism is a defense mechanism against Communism." This concept he borrowed from the Nazis, who originated it. For that reason, when Father Coughlin expounded the "defense mechanism" theory in his radio address of November 20, 1938, he was hailed in Germany. "The German hero in America for the moment is the Rev. Charles E. Coughlin because of his radio speech representing national socialism as a defense front against bolshevism," said a dispatch from Berlin by Otto D. Tolischus, a staff correspondent for the New York *Times*, November 27, 1938.

of these excesses as evils which must be eradicated from our social soil. For many weeks, I have been expressing the opinion that Nazism is only a defense mechanism against Communism . I believe the time is now opportune for Americans and Christians to erect a defense mechanism against both of them.[10] Unless we are successful in accomplishing this , we must content ourselves to permit these two social irregularities to fight it out . Both are adamant, and each is determined his side will conquer. To the victor we [11] will be forced to surrender our rights, our ideals, our liberties.

Thus, if Americanism and Christianity are opposed to both Nazism and Communism, the time has come for true Americans and true Christians to organize against both, to act against both, and this active organization should be characterized not so much by negative opposition as by a positive program. Let us be honest with ourselves. In the first instance, Communists and their supporters have real grievances. So have the Nazis. Communism, which antedates Nazism, complains about forced unemployment. It cries out against less than living wages for the laborer, against the huge profits for the rich. It condemns the modern system of capitalism, with its legalized usury, its burdens and taxes, its monopolies of industry, and its commercial wars.

No one who sympathizes with the poor and who loves social justice, disagrees with the Communists in these complaints . Long before the subject of Communism was broached by Karl Marx, Christian leaders voiced these same

[10] Democracy as the alternative to both Communism and Nazism is apparently ruled out by Father Coughlin. In view of his expressed attitude toward democracy, this is hardly surprising.

[11] Father Coughlin's use of the Plain Folks Device here is an attempt to disassociate himself from the Nazis, who cheered every mention of his name at the Bund Garden rally. He wants his listeners to believe that he is just one of them, and not a Nazi sympathizer to whom they may some day be forced to surrender their "rights, ideals, and liberties."

complaints. If we hope to liquidate Communism, we must continue to condemn these social injustices 🖐, we must liquidate the causes that beget Communists, causes which characterize ☞ our present economic and political order. Communism is not opposed to us 👆 because it finds justifiable ⚜ reason to complain about the heavy and unnecessary cross 🖐 which was placed upon the shoulders of the laboring man by the Pontius Pilates of politics 🖐 🎩, together with the high priests of international finance 🖐 🎩. It is condemned because the remedies it advocates to alleviate the sufferings ⚜ of the poor will leave the poor in a worse 🖐 condition than the one from which they are endeavoring to escape.

What are some of the Communistic remedies? Because Communists blame governments and politicians, at least in part ☞, for the sad plight 🖐 of the workingman and the farmer, they say, "Let's take over the government." Because they blamed the industrialists for low wages 🖐, unsanitary 🖐 working conditions, periods of layoff, together with the speed-up system 🖐, they say, "Let's take over the factories." Because they blame the Church ☞ [12] preaching the gospel which protects bad 🖐 government, bad 🖐 finance, and bad 🖐 industrial economics, they say, "Let's abolish the churches."

These are the three major ingredients ☞ which are compounded into the pill known as Communism, a pill 🖐 that is sugar-coated 🖐 with hopes and promises. Fortunately for America, Russia was the first sick patient 🖐 to summon Doctor Karl Marx to her bedside. Russia swallowed the pill 🖐. The entire world 👆 is aware of the pains 🖐 and distress 🖐 which that poor 🖐 country is suffering 🖐 as a result of her

[12] Father Coughlin is only partly correct here. The Communists have pointed out that in Czarist Russia the established church supported the Czarist régime. This was their excuse for destroying the established church. However, they did not abolish all churches, for some churches are still open in the Soviet Union. The Communist opposition to religion, as distinguished from their opposition to the old Russian Orthodox Church, springs from the Marxist doctrine that religion is essentially based upon superstition.

experiment. It is true 🔅 that the Russian Revolution abolished a bad 🦷 government, but what did Russia gain? Having gladly 🔅 lost the Czars, she gained Lenin, Trotsky, Stalin—the dictators 🦷 memorable for their ravages 🦷 and their mass murders 🦷. It is true 🔅 that the laboring and peasant classes of Czaristic Russia were exploited under a usurious 🦷 capitalistic system ⚫. Now these same people are slaves 🦷 of the state. It is true 🔅 that too many churchmen in Russia supported both the despotism 🦷 of the Czars and failed to condemn vigorously the capitalism of the financial lords 🦷. Now the Russian people have preached to them the gospel of hate 🦷, have materialism 🦷, have atheism 🦷, with no hopeful outlook beyond the grave.

Knowing all these things, America is very disinclined to summon Doctor Karl Marx to her bedside, because America knows that the cure effected by the little red pill 🦷 of Communism is worse 🦷 than the disease 🦷 ⚫. Germany profited by this experience ⚫.[13] Following the World War, the German people suffered from the same ⚫ ailments 🦷 which afflicted 🦷 their neighbors in Russia. At Germany's bedside stood Doctor Karl Marx. Carefully he diagnosed the dread disease 🦷. The ravages of unemployment 🦷 had spread throughout the entire body, the infection of debt 🦷 was manifest in every vein and artery, the fever of exploitation 🦷 was evidenced in her bloodshot eyes. In despair, Germany was almost at the point of swallowing the little red pill 🦷 ⚫, when a group of specialists 🔅, Doctors Rosenberg, Goering, Goebbels, and Hitler, storm-trooped into the bedroom, evicted the quack 🦷 Doctor Marx, and administered to the patient the sparkling, candy-coated brown pill 🦷.[14] These specialists 🔅

[13] Here Father Coughlin is going back to his idea that Germany adopted Nazism to forestall Communism. As we have pointed out, that is the official Nazi doctrine, but it definitely is not one on which many disinterested authorities are agreed.

[14] How close Germany came to "swallowing the little red pill" of Communism is perhaps indicated by the fact that of the 608 deputies

did not disagree with Doctor Marx in the causes of Germany's affliction ⚕. Their remedy ▨, however, was compounded from social chemicals which were not quite so ▨ fatal in their immediate effects.

For example, the German specialists ▨ agreed that religion ▨ was necessary for the restoration of national health ▨ to the sick patient ⚕ ⬚, but these doctors were quick to add that only that brand of the Christian religion would be tolerated which surrendered ⚕ the education of children to the state, and which agreed to refrain from teaching any doctrine or expounding any policy contrary to the doctrines and policies of the state ⬚.[15] The little brown pill ⚕ banished unemployment, limited profits for the industrialists, liquidated debts and capitalistic exploitation ⬚.[16] However, the partially recovered

elected to the German Reichstag on July 31, 1932, only 89 were Communists. The Communist Party had a very long way to go in Germany before it could even hope to gain power.

[15] The Nazi attitude toward religion is best indicated, perhaps, by what the Nazis have done to religious organizations in Germany since gaining power in 1933. Here are some headlines from the New York Times:

1933: "Campaign Against Catholicism, Pope Launched"
"Hitler Confidant, Mueller, Made Reich Bishop"
1934: "League for Free Religious Associations Closed"
"Christianized Jews Restricted to Ghetto Churches"
"Dictatorship of Protestants Assumed by Nazis"
1935: "Control of Church Finances Seized by Regime"
"1,500 Pastors Confined in Their Own Homes"
"54 Societies of Nuns and Monks Raided"
"Activities of Religious Youth Groups Curtailed"
1936: "150 Leaders of Catholic Youth Groups Arrested"
"Editorials of Religious Journals Muzzled"
1937: "Church Attendance by Children Restricted"
"Catholic Printing Plant Seized by Police"
"Storm Troops Receive Paganistic Instruction"
"Rosenberg Announced Plan to Absorb Christianity"
"Christ Was Anti-Semitic, Streicher Announces"

[16] Father Coughlin takes Nazi propaganda at face value. Disinterested authorities like the *London Economist* or Paul Mallon, syndicated

⬚ patient began to suffer from the high blood pressure of racialism and partial paralysis ⬚ in the regions of political liberty.

Thus, it is conceded ⬚ that both Doctors Marx and Hitler, together with their assistants, were more or less accurate ⬚ in discovering the nature of the diseases which afflicted Russia and Germany. Their diagnosis is very applicable to America ⬚, but it is my belief that America, sick as she is ⬚, is reluctant to swallow either the red pill of Communism ⬚ or the brown pill of Nazism ⬚.

I speak of these things in association with the Bund meeting held last Monday night in Madison Square Garden. It is noteworthy that Communist meetings have been in vogue for many years, and have created little or no comment ⬚.[17] Now

newspaper columnist who recently conducted a study of Nazi economy for the Hearst papers, take another view of the results of Nazism upon German labor and business. See, in this connection, "Caught Between 'Must' and 'Can't'—The Story of the German Business Man," by Rothay Reynolds in the New York *Times*, April 23, 1939. Or, witness these headlines from the New York *Times*:

> "Unions Placed Under Supervision of Police"
> "Strikes, Collective Bargaining Forbidden by Law"
> "Labor Service Made Compulsory for Youths"
> "Low Pay, High Prices, Cause Widespread Discontent"
> "Goebbels Warns Against Hope of Wage Rise"
> "Catholic Workers Ousted from Labor Front"
> "Speed-up of Workers Necessitated by Rearmament"
> "Labor Service Camp Enrollment Lengthened"

Professor Robert A. Brady of the University of California, summarizing the effect of Nazism on business, has concluded that wages are below the depression level, that living costs have increased, that hours of work have been lengthened, that labor has been regimented, that industry has been concentrated into fewer hands, that profits have increased, that taxes have doubled, and that the middle class is dying out. (See "Five Years of Hitler," published by the American Council on Public Affairs, New York City.)

[17] Father Coughlin should read the Hearst papers, the Chicago *Tribune*, the Los Angeles *Times*, or any other of the hundreds of American newspapers which have discussed Communism for years. Or else, he

that the Communists are openly opposed 🔲, and very vigorously opposed, not only by Nazis, who formed only a small segment 🔲 [18] of last Monday's meeting, but also by thousands of anti-Communists who are not Nazi-minded 🔲, but who joined the Bundists in protest, it is a most opportune time for Americans 🔲 to enter into this contest 🔲, a contest which will determine whether Christian Americanism 🔲 will prevail, or some foreign ism, dominated by an insignificant 🔲, will be inflicted 🔲 upon us 🔲 🔲.

We 🔲 cannot successfully fight Communism by being negative 🔲. We will not be satisfied to destroy Communism at the expense 🔲 of accepting Nazism. We 🔲 must be positive 🔲, first, by recognizing the social injustices 🔲 which gave rise to Communism and Nazism; and, second, by uniting our forces behind a sound program of reform 🔲 which is in harmony 🔲 with our Constitution and our Christianity 🔲. Millions of American citizens 🔲, now followers either of the Communistic or Nazi cause,[19] once this program is presented, will abandon the red flag and the swastika as soon as they can discover an active 🔲, sound 🔲 program, in harmony 🔲 with the Stars and Stripes 🔲 and the Cross of Christ 🔲, a program which, if reduced to action, will liquidate the social,

should read the reports of the Dies Committee or the Fish Committee. He would discover that Communist activities *have* created more than a little comment.

[18] Another step in the "softening" technique. First, Father Coughlin called the meeting "Nazi." Then, it became "predominately pro-Nazi." Now, it is attended by only a small group of Nazis with the overwhelming majority of the participants neither Nazi nor pro-Nazi, but just anti-Communist.

[19] It is difficult to see how Father Coughlin counts "millions" of Communists and Nazis in the United States. The Communist Party, U. S. A., has between 75,000 and 90,000 members. The German-American Bund comprises between 6,600 and 8,300 individuals, according to a recent report of the Department of Justice. The Silver Shirt Legion has between 5,000 and 10,000 members. The other communist and fascist organizations are even smaller. For example the Communist Party Opposition is said to have about 400 members.

the industrial, the political, and the financial abuses ⚑ which are responsible 👁 for our national misery ⚑.

What principles should be incorporated in such a plan? First, liberty of conscience and of education ⚘. A man and his family must be guaranteed the right to worship his God when and how he pleases.[20] A father must be assured that his children belong to him, and not to the state, and therefore that he has the right to educate his children either in public or private schools.[21]

Second, a just ⚘ living ⚘ annual wage must be assured to every breadwinner who is able and willing to work. The policy of paying a man only when he works, at so much per hour, was, perhaps, satisfactory before the advent of mass production machinery. Today, that policy is as obsolete ⚑ as the one-horse shay.

Third, certain public resources should be nationalized, in the sense that either Federal or State governments may develop transportation, power, and light, through the agency of politically free ⚘ corporations, but not in the sense that Federal or State governments should monopolize ⚑ public utilities to the exclusion of private corporations.[22]

Fourth, private ownership of property should not only be guaranteed, but should be cultivated ⚘ by the Government. Particularly I have reference to the homes of laborers and small farmers, which should be tax-exempt up to a certain valuation. No nation which can point to a widespread ownership of homes, needs worry about the advances of Communism or Nazism.

[20] He already is.

[21] Parents already have that right. They can send their children to public, private, or parochial schools, as they wish.

[22] Just what Father Coughlin means by "politically free corporations" would be difficult to say. Disregarding this Glittering Generality however, what he proposes is precisely what already exists. Thus, we have municipally owned power plants in the United States, and we have the federally owned T.V.A., but at the same time we have privately owned public utilities.

Fifth, the control of private property for the public good ▧ should be an integral part of this program. Everyone recognizes a man who owns a motor car, for example, may not use it as he pleases, because his property must be subject to the control for common good ▧. He may not drive it on the crowded side of a thoroughfare at sixty miles an hour. The public good ▧ also demands that they who own factories may not operate them to the detriment of the public good ▧, nor may owners operate them on the principle of production for profit only ▧. It seems to me that production for use at a profit to all ▧ is a sounder ▧ principle, even though this principle will demand a limitation of profits.[23]

Sixth, it is evident ▱ that factories cannot operate, and that living wages cannot be paid to employees, unless an ample ▧ purchasing power is enjoyed by the nation at large to purchase the products of field and factory. Hence, this program incorporates in its platform the principle that Congress shall coin and regulate the value of money,[24] so that there will be an ample sufficiency ▧ in the hands of the purchasing public, to the end that the law of supply and demand will not be obstructed by any artificial barrier of debt money or lack of wealth money ▱.

[23] More Glittering Generalities. Everyone recognizes and has long recognized that private property must be "controlled for the public good." It was in keeping with such principles that Congress passed the Sherman Anti-Trust Act, the Clayton Act, the Federal Reserve Act, the Securities and Exchange Law, and the Wages and Hours Act. The question is not whether laws regulating business should be enacted. Such laws have been enacted by Congress throughout our history. The question is, *what laws?* Father Coughlin talks in Glittering Generalities but gives no specific answer.

The Nazi Party in Germany, incidentally, uses the same Glittering Generalities. "We demand ruthless *prosecution of those whose activities are injurious* to the common interest," reads the official Nazi program.

[24] Again, Father Coughlin's vagueness of expression makes analysis difficult. The Constitution of the United States already reads: "The Congress shall have the power . . . To coin money, regulate the value thereof . . ."

Seventh, it shall be the business of Government to keep the cost of living on an even keel. This means, if you will, that prices must be regulated, if not fixed, so that profits ▧ will be assured for all—profits ▧ for the working man [25] as well as for the manufacturer. To my mind, it is a social injustice ⚘ for Government to permit ▣ and condone ▣ the manipulation ⚘ of prices ▣, and, consequently, of commercial values. It is evident ▣ in a case where the home owner buys a house for ten thousand dollars in 1928, and, for no other cause ▣ than for a financial cause ▣ called deflation, this purchaser sees the value of his house shrink to three thousand dollars in 1933. Deflation is a social injustice ⚘ which results in the confiscation ⚘ of private property.

Witness the confiscation ⚘ in the case of a farmer or factory home owner. If the former buys a farm for ten thousand dollars when wheat is a dollar a bushel, he owes ten thousand bushels of wheat. If the price of wheat drops to fifty cents a bushel, he owes twenty thousand bushels of wheat on the loan he obtained to purchase his farm. This means he must plow twice as many furrows, plant twice as many bushels, work twice as many hours. In the case of the poor factory worker who buys a home when work is plentiful at a dollar an hour, he finds it impossible to pay off the mortgage on his property in periods of deflation, which are always identified with periods of unemployment and depleted wages ▣.[26]

[25] Father Coughlin apparently is somewhat confused over the meaning of the word "profit." In the social and personal sense the word means any benefit or gain derived. In that sense workers almost invariably profit from labor since they do receive some reward even if the reward be insufficient as measured by their services. In the *economic* sense, however, the word profit has an entirely different meaning. Webster's Universal Dictionary says: "Profit—the advantage or gain resulting to the owner of capital from its employment in any undertaking; the difference between the original cost and selling price of anything; excess of value received beyond expenditure; pecuniary gain." Thus, by definition, only the capitalist can earn a profit.

[26] Although it may be true, as Father Coughlin says, that "periods of deflation—are always identified with periods of unemployment and de-

Congress is responsible for deflations 〔•〕.[27] Congress must pass legislation to outlaw this social injustice 🖐.[28] Otherwise, both the farmer and the laborer will surrender their properties to the mortgage holder as a result of this neglect 🖐.

Eighth, the chief industry of this or of any other nation is agriculture. All industry and all citizens depend upon the farmer not only for food, but for every product of the soil which enters into the fabrication of most things we use. I am using the word "farmer" in a broad sense.[29] Hence, any financial or economic system which does not guarantee the cost of production plus a fair profit,[30] is an unsound 🖐 economic system. There are thirty million farmers and farmers' dependents in America. If this economic group is unable to purchase the products of the factory, then at least thirty million workmen will be paralyzed 〔•〕.[31] Thus, solidarity ✧ or class co-operation ✧ [32] is an essential to the economic well-

pleted wages," it does not, of course, follow that deflation *causes* unemployment. On the contrary, deflation and unemployment are both aspects of the workings of the economic cycle.

[27] How?

[28] What legislation?

[29] Very broad, indeed.

[30] How?

[31] Father Coughlin, to make his point, has created here an unprecedented situation. Never in the history of the United States have we had 30,000,000 unemployed. And what, precisely, does Father Coughlin mean when he speaks of the farmers "being unable to purchase the products of the factory"? Does he mean that not one farmer in the whole of the United States would be able to purchase one factory product? The situation is utterly inconceivable. And, supposing it were to exist, where does Father Coughlin get his figure of 30,000,000 unemployed?

[32] "Class co-operation" is the guiding doctrine of both the German Nazi and the Italian Fascist States. It was used as the excuse for destroying all political parties but the Nazi Party in Germany and the Fascist Party in Italy. Numerous independent political parties made for conflict in government, said the Nazis and Fascists, when "co-operation" should be the goal. Similarly, "class co-operation" was the reason for abolishing the independent labor unions, the establishment of the German Labor Front and the Italian Corporative system.

being ⬛ of America, and this class co-operation begins on the farm, where raw materials originate.[33]

Nine, this program must incorporate the right of labor to organize.[34] This is a natural right ⬛ which must be protected by Government.[35] I do not mean that labor should organize only for its own selfish interests ⬛. Labor should organize both for its own protection, and for the common good of the nation ⬛, on the basis that capital cannot do without labor, and labor cannot do without capital. This principle should not be misinterpreted to mean that labor should organize to destroy ⬛ private property or to set up a proletarian dictatorship.[36] Nor does this principle exclude the right of capital to organize.[37] Neither capital nor labor should organize against each other, because social justice ⬛ must be meted out to all without exception.[38]

[33] Who on the farm co-operates with whom? The sharecropper with the absentee landlord? The farm owner with the hired hand? And how do they co-operate? Does Father Coughlin want the farmer and the farm hand to co-operate in producing food? They already do. In fact, they always have.

[34] Labor already has this right, under the Wagner Act.

[35] It already is "protected by the Government."

[36] Does Father Coughlin mean to imply that either the American Federation of Labor or the Congress of Industrial Organizations or any of the independent unions are organized for that purpose?

[37] Capital already has that right.

[38] Father Coughlin has just finished saying that labor should organize "for its own protection." Father Coughlin, it would therefore seem, recognizes that some employers constantly seek to lower wages, to increase hours, and to worsen conditions of work, in general. Indeed, Father Coughlin earlier in this speech has implied that all, or nearly all, employers are guilty of such practices. He spoke of "low wages, unsanitary working conditions, the speed-up system." Now, how can labor organize to protect itself except by organizing *against* such employers? Moreover, how can labor organize *with* such employers? Is Father Coughlin euphemistically urging the establishment in the United States of something like the Nazi Labor Front, which includes both employers and employees, with the employers in executive positions and the employees making up the rank and file? How would such an organization

Tenth, under the modern capitalistic system, our money or credit, the common denominator of all economic activity, is issued and controlled by private corporations ⟨·⟩. Billions upon billions of dollars of non-productive loans have been made to our Government by the private creators of money. On the other hand, some loans were made for productive purposes. For example, I cite the loans made for the construction of the T.V.A., the Boulder Dam, and the flood relief projects. They were productive loans. Other loans were made for non-productive purposes, out of which no future wealth can be obtained. I give as an example the loans made to dig shell holes, to destroy cities, to plow under cotton, to pay farmers for what they did not produce.

Now, both these productive and non-productive loans are represented by bonds—bonds obtained from the Government either by the private corporations which originated the loans or by other corporations which, in turn, purchased these bonds. Radical ⟨⟩ as this may sound, I am of the opinion that the non-productive loans should be canceled entirely ⟨·⟩, that the bonds representing them should be destroyed ⟨·⟩, but that the productive loans represented by bonds should not be destroyed, but should be retained, but subject to taxation ⟨·⟩.[39]

Eleven, at present, a great ⟨⟩ portion of our Federal and

in the United States offer any more protection to workers than it does in Germany? For what has been happening to German labor, see Footnote 16.

[39] Neither Father Coughlin, nor anybody else, including the President of the United States and the Secretary of the Treasury, could divide the outstanding U. S. Government bonds into two such groups: those issued to raise money for destructive purposes, and those issued for constructive purposes. Government bonds are rarely issued for any *specific* purpose, *except to meet the Government deficit*. The Liberty bonds *were* issued for the specific purpose of financing the World War. That is true. However, they were an exception. Also exceptional are the so-called "quasi governmental bonds," like the H.O.L.C. issues. There are, for example, no A.A.A. bonds, in spite of what Father Coughlin says.

State taxation is predicated upon the medium of consumer taxes. I mean, the tax on bread, milk, medicine, clothing, and the necessities of life. Entirely out of proportion does the poor man and the unemployed man contribute toward this consumers' tax. Thus I believe that consumer taxation should be levied on the principle of one's capacity to pay and on the basis of ownership, not necessarily on the basis of consumption, when it is concerned with the necessities of life.[40]

Twelve, already our nation is overrun with bureaucrats.[41] Literally millions of persons are working for the Government, which is engaged in public works, in building highways, bridges, canals, flood dams, and so forth. Oh! but a plenitude of abuses ☞, both political and social, have resulted therefrom, because the Government directly regimented ☞ ☞ this army of workmen, and pays them a less than living wage ☞ ☞.[42] As a result, inefficiency ☞, paternalism ☞ and a low standard of morale ☞ results. Moreover, under our present system of political paternalism ☞, we have degenerated ☞ to our present low standard of economic life,[43] which now threatens our

[40] How does Father Coughlin hope to achieve this? Does he advocate that people in one income bracket pay one tax on every article they buy, while people in another, higher bracket pay additional taxes on the same article? Would not that make it almost impossible to carry on trade, for would it not mean that people would have to sit down and figure out the excise or sales tax for their present income level every time they made a purchase? Or does Father Coughlin mean to advocate that all excise taxes be abolished, that graduated income taxes be relied upon for Government revenue? If the latter, why does he use the phrase "consumer taxes"? Why doesn't he say "income taxes"?

[41] Yet, Father Coughlin urges that our Government take on additional functions, like fixing prices, which naturally would necessitate an even larger Government bureaucracy.

[42] Workers on P.W.A. are paid the prevailing wage in their industry. This means that, at worst, they receive far more than German workers. At best, they receive union wages—the highest wages for similar labor in the world. As for W.P.A. workers, even they receive more than German workers.

[43] Still the highest in the world.

democracy [44] and our Christianity. Millions of advocates 👍,[45] either of Nazism or Communism, are prone to blame this method of Government upon democracy itself.[46] Consequently, I advocate a simplification 🌊 of Government [47] for the preservation of democracy 🌊.

Thirteen, never in the history of this nation or of any other nation has the man behind the plow or the man at the lathe voted for war 👁.[48] To those of us who have enjoyed the opportunity to visit the peoples of Europe and elsewhere ⚭, it is evident that no people wants war. Those who plan wars, those who spread propaganda to incite wars, they who profit by wars are seldom they who fight wars. They who influence legislators to conscript the flower of our youth, to tear young husbands from their wives and babies, and to confiscate the most precious treasure owned by loving mothers—I mean their sons—they are the ones who want war.[49] Wars are no accidents. They are planned 👁.[50] They are planned by those whose minds are obsessed 🖐 with commercial greed 🖐 and international domination 🖐.

Consequently, I lay it down as a principle of social justice 🌊 that, in event of any war, in event of the confiscation 🖐

[44] In view of what Father Coughlin has said about democracy, his sincerity here is open to question.

[45] On what does Father Coughlin base this estimate?

[46] Nevertheless, contrast wages paid on W.P.A. with the daily wage of 25 pfennigs (about 10 cents) plus room and board received by German youth in the Labor Service camps.

[47] How? Does Father Coughlin advocate the discontinuance of W.P.A. and P.W.A.? What Government bureaus would he like to eliminate? Moreover, see Footnote 43.

[48] They have never had an opportunity to. However, there *have* been popular wars.

[49] It would have been impossible to list all the propaganda devices used in this sentence. Two or three symbols would have been needed for almost every word. For example, "precious treasures," "loving mothers," etc.

[50] Specifically, what individuals planned the World War? Or does Father Coughlin believe in the "Kaiser's war guilt" theory?

of human life under the title of conscription, there shall not be issued any war bonds redeemable at any future date, nor shall there be issued any war loans repayable at any future time. What profit does the soldier in the front trench acquire out of the grime, the vermin, and the wound which he receives? What profit should those who remain at home acquire? They contribute no more than does the soldier who risks his life, and let them gain no more. Let them be paid no more, be they banker, industrialist, Congressman, President, or powder manufacturer.[51]

Fourteenth and final, let the sanctity 🔲 of human rights 🔲 be preferred to the sanctity 🔲 of property or financial rights 🔲, and let the Government's chief concern be toward the poor 🔲.

In all, however, social justice 🔲 demands class co-operation 🔲 and is opposed to class conflict 🔲. It is predicated upon the general principle that there can be no prosperity for one class in America unless there is prosperity for all classes 🔲. And, from a religious viewpoint 🔲 🔲, the foundation 🔲 of this entire program is the Christian 🔲 teaching that whatsoever we do to the least of Christ's little ones, we do unto him 🔲.

All together 🔲, my friends 🔲, these principles are a platform for Christian American 🔲 🔲 action. I remind you again of last Monday's meeting at Madison Square Garden. What a sad commentary 🔲 it was that such a meeting should commemorate the birthday of George Washington. While we 🔲 admit 🔲 that Nazism is a defense mechanism against Communism 🔲, nevertheless we Americans 🔲, who are determined to sacrifice everything 🔲 rather than accept Communism, we 🔲 will never be content to league ourselves

[51] Surprisingly like the Nazi program again is this demand of Father Coughlin's. The Nazi program reads: "We demand therefore ruthless *confiscation of all war gains.*"

with the Nazis in our nation .[52] Must we import a foreign program? Must we submit to a foreign ideology to protect us from the hammer and sickle? Such thoughts are absurd.

But let us not deceive ourselves. It is impossible to talk Communism out of existence. The sword of rhetoric will flash harmlessly against the hard backs of unemployment, of less than living wages, of confiscatory taxation, and of the other evils which are associated with modern capitalism and its exploitation. Believe me, if I criticize modern capitalism, I am not criticizing the capitalists themselves, who have contributed so much toward the development of America. I am simply drawing to their attention certain abuses which are clamoring for redress.

This, then, is no time for us to divide our forces, be we rich or poor, Catholic or Protestant, Democratic or Republican. This is the time for us to stand together, a time when minds must meet and evolve a common program for common action, as we unite to preserve Americanism and Christianity against the militant forces which are advancing to destroy it. If you believe in these words, be not content to receive them and then forget them. Be resolute in discussing them with your family, your business associates, and your organizations. Nothing can be gained by leaguing ourselves with any organization that is engaged in agitating racial animosities or propagating racial hatreds. Organizations which stand upon such platforms are immoral, and their policies are, at the best, only negative.

[52] However, Father Coughlin has already "leagued himself with the Nazis in our nation." His followers have joined with the German-American Bund in picketing radio stations which refuse to broadcast his speeches. His weekly newspaper, *Social Justice*, was on sale at the Bund rally in the Garden. His name, according to newspaper reports, was cheered more wildly than any other by those who attended the rally. And, to quote Mr. Tolischus again, "The German hero in America . . . is the Rev. Charles E. Coughlin . . ."

Ours ♌ must be a moral ♒ platform from which there is preached ⛎ a positive ♒ policy based upon the principles of religion ♒ ⛎ and of patriotism ♒. For God ⛎ and country ⛎ ♒, for Christ ⛎ and the flag ⛎ ♒—that is our motto as we prepare for action, for Christian American ⛎ ♒ action, which is neither anti-German, anti-Italian, nor anti-Semitic ⛉. Any negative ♑ policy is destined to failure. Only a positive policy ♒ can hope to succeed. Unified ♌ action on a common ♌ program for God ⛎ and country is more necessary now than at any other period in the history of our civilization ⛉.

XII. And Now?

FROM our descriptions of the seven ABC's of Propaganda Analysis and our lengthy illustrations of the seven Propaganda Devices, some may conclude that it takes a lot of fact grubbing to come to a satisfactory conclusion regarding some project a propagandist is trying to "sell" us. Some may even have gone so far by this time as to say, "It's too much work. I'll take the advice of some expert I trust and let it go at that."

This defeatism is far from being justified. It is true that we have thought it necessary to illustrate thoroughly the ways in which the Propaganda Devices are being utilized to distort our opinions. It is not necessary, however, to analyze scientifically all that we hear over the radio or read in our daily papers. Our purpose has been to help our readers to become more alert to the tricks of the propagandist's trade, to encourage all believers in democracy to test *samples* of the offerings of all propagandists as best we can in order to weigh the merits of all their offerings, and *above all to suspend our judgments until we have heard as many sides of any issue as we can.*

The search for truth has been age long. The quest for some certainty as to what is the best next step in social policy has preoccupied the outstanding thinkers of the world for many, many generations. The fruits of this search have given mankind a civilization of marvelous complexity and with a multitude of opportunities for many people despite our civilization's maladjustments, our unemployment, wars, recurrent depressions, etc.

This search for truth has been vastly stimulated by the spread and preservation of the democratic way of life. Only in a democracy do scientists, artists, technicians, philosophers, and ministers of religious sects have the freedom that permits them to strive for more and more accurate approximations of that eternal earthly goal of man, the truth.

But democracy, as we have said, not only carries with it the greatest of human opportunities, it also places upon us all the greatest obligations. And these obligations are more complex and exacting than were the obligations it placed upon our parents or upon any other preceding generation. The challenge to democracy in the world today is for us to face and shoulder these obligations more adequately than ever before. This challenge to democracy is for Americans and all others who believe in it to keep on making their own decisions, to make ever wiser decisions concerning our problems, and to keep on inviting free— even though dangerous—choices among the alternatives presented to us.

Dictatorships *promise* stability, security, and easy answers to many pressing problems but they can appear to fulfill these promises *only in the short run*. Dictatorships, once established, very shortly make decisions which do not yield security, decisions which crush the individual and drive on to the annihilation in war of society itself.

Our seven ABC's of Propaganda Analysis and our seven Propaganda Devices are offered therefore as workable means for aiding Americans to preserve their freedom of choice and with it their other freedoms embodied so largely in the expression, freedom of propaganda: freedom of speech and assembly, of the press, and of religion. In closing, then, let us merely sum up the spirit of our seven ABC's and seven devices in the following statements:

Don't be stampeded.

Beware of your own prejudices.

Suspend your judgment until more sides of the issue are presented.

Analyze them.

Some Reading Suggestions

THE MANY who will want to learn more about the fine art of propaganda have a plentiful supply of interesting and useful books and other publications to which they may turn.

New bulletins are no longer published by the Institute for Propaganda Analysis, but a great many libraries contain the four volumes (1937–1942) of *Propaganda Analysis* that were issued. These volumes still have freshness and relevance to the current scene. Reprints and microfilms of them may be obtained from University Microfilms, Ann Arbor, Michigan.

The following annotated bibliographies on propaganda and related subjects are useful:

Harold D. Lasswell, Ralph D. Casey, and Bruce L. Smith, eds., *Propaganda and Promotional Activities* (Minneapolis: University of Minnesota Press, 1935). This work also includes important introductory essays.

Bruce L. Smith, Harold D. Lasswell, and Ralph D. Casey, eds., *Propaganda, Communication, and Public Opinion* (Princeton: Princeton University Press, 1946). This "comprehensive reference guide" also includes four essays by its editors.

Scott M. Cutlip, ed., *A Public Relations Bibliography* (Madison: University of Wisconsin Press, 1960). Even though the title focuses on the propaganda "producer," this annotated bibliography is quite broad and helpful in its coverage of "consumer's" interests.

More recent bibliographies, reviews, and abstracts of interesting items may be found in the following periodicals:

Journalism Quarterly
Public Opinion Quarterly
Psychological Abstracts
Sociological Abstracts

The annotated bibliographies that follow include useful books on propaganda, discussion methods, and education for democracy:

TOWARDS AN UNDERSTANDING OF PROPAGANDA

Berelson, Bernard, and Morris Janowitz, eds., *Reader in Public Opinion and Communication,* 2nd ed. (New York: Free Press, 1966). Excerpts from the work of many leading writers. Somewhat more focused on the problems of propaganda producers than on those of the consumer.

Doob, Leonard W., *Public Opinion and Propaganda,* 2nd ed. (Hamden, Conn.: Archon Books, 1966). Consideration of propaganda as a means of social control, a method with which individuals and groups work for their own interests, and a problem with which individuals and society as a whole must contend.

Ellul, Jacques, *Propaganda: The Formation of Men's Attitudes,* transl. from the French by Konrad Kellen and Jean Lerner (New York: Alfred A. Knopf, 1965). A discussion of how propagandists exploit what we have already learned in order to achieve their own goals. He tries "to show people the extreme effectiveness of the weapon used against them, to rouse them to defend themselves."

Institute for Propaganda Analysis, Inc., *The Group Leader's Guide to Propaganda Analysis* (New York, 1938). Experimental study materials for use in high schools, colleges, and adult study groups.

Katz, Daniel, Dorwin Cartwright, Samuel Eldersveld, and A. McC. Lee, eds., *Public Opinion and Propaganda: A Book of Readings* (New York: Dryden Press and the Society for the Psychological Study of Social Issues, 1954). The nature, functions, processes, and dynamics of public opinion formation and change. The identification and measurement of public opinion and propaganda and their effects. The focus is in part on the consumer's problems and in part on the producer's.

Lee, Alfred McClung, *How to Understand Propaganda* (New York: Rinehart & Co., 1952). A consumer perspective on propaganda: messages to publics, the propagandists, the propaganda instruments, the use of organizations, how propagandists try to use your mind, and a general view. Throughout the emphasis is on: What can individuals do about propaganda?

Lippmann, Walter, *Public Opinion* (1922; New York: Macmillan Co., 1960). A famous book on propaganda and public opinion by a famous journalist. Shows the dependence of opinion on prejudice and other factors that color our judgment. His discussion of "stereotypes" is widely admired and quoted.

MacDougall, Curtis D., *Understanding Public Opinion*, 2nd ed. (Dubuque, Iowa: William C. Brown & Co., 1966). A basic college test. He explores definitions and fundamental principles, relates public opinion and propaganda to culture, and explores opinion media.

McGinniss, Joe, *The Selling of the President: 1968* (New

York: Trident Press, 1969). This is a candid and exciting report from behind the scenes on how Richard Nixon was advertised, given public "exposure," had his "public image" designed and constructed. Sometimes shocking, often funny, always readable.

Packard, Vance, *The Hidden Persuaders* (New York: Pocket Books, 1957). Use of propaganda "to channel our unthinking habits, our purchasing decisions, and our thought processes by the use of insights gleaned from psychiatry and the social sciences." Sensational but useful.

Ross, Irwin, *The Image Merchants: The Fabulous World of Public Relations* (Garden City, N.Y.: Doubleday & Co., 1959). The personal and business careers of propagandists. Characterizations of the some "100,000 people busily creating, restructuring, and projecting preconceived images of clients who range from corporations to private individuals."

Schettler, Clarence, *Public Opinion in American Society* (New York: Harper & Brothers, 1960). A basic university text by a mature sociologist. It deals extensively with propaganda and propaganda media.

Sorensen, Thomas C., *Word War: The Story of American Propaganda* (New York: Harper & Row, 1968). Foreword by Robert F. Kennedy. Running story of United States propaganda in both World Wars and since.

Sumner, William Graham, *Folkways: A Study of the Sociological Importance of Usages, Manners, Customs, Mores, and Morals* (1906; New York: New American Library, 1960). After more than two generations, this book is still widely read and even more widely quoted. Chapters I and V are especially recommended for the student of public opinion.

Ward, Henshaw, *Builders of Delusion* (Indianapolis: Bobbs-

Merrill, 1931). A satirical "Tour Among Our Best Minds," an analysis of competing theories or propagandas on many significant issues. Easy reading, still very timely, and highly provocative.

ON RELIGIOUS SECTS AND PROPAGANDA

Abrams, Ray H., *Preachers Present Arms* (Scottdale, Pa.: Herald Press, 1969, re-issue). The involvement of clergymen in pro-war propaganda.

Chalmers, David M., *Hooded Americanism: The History of the Ku Klux Klan* (Chicago: Quadrangle, 1968).

Jackson, Kenneth T., *Ku Klux Klan in the City: 1915-1930* (New York: Oxford University Press, 1967).

Konvitz, Milton R., *Religious Liberty and Conscience* (New York: Viking Press, 1969). A discussion of constitutional guarantees and court decisions having to do with religious freedom.

Mecklin, John M., *Ku Klux Klan: A Study of the American Mind* (1924; New York: Russell and Russell, 1963).

Myers, Gustavus, *History of Bigotry in the United States,* ed. and material added by H. M. Christman (New York: Capricorn Books, 1960). From the crusades against the Puritans and Quakers through the anti-Masonic and anti-Catholic and anti-Negro excesses of the nineteenth century to the hate campaigns of the twentieth. A guide and a challenge to the democratic.

Trelease, Allen W., *White Terror: The Ku Klux Klan Conspiracy and Southern Reconstruction* (New York: Harper & Row, 1971).

White, Andrew D., *History of the Warfare of Science With Theology in Christendom* (New York: Dover Publications, re-issue, 1896 ed., 2 vols). A classic interpretation of a major conflict which for centuries gave rise to propaganda in all its manifestations and still does.

ON DEMOCRACY AND FREEDOM OF DISCUSSION

The Declaration of Independence
The Constitution of the United States of America
Anderson, Walt, ed., *The Age of Protest* (Pacific Palisades, Calif.: Goodyear Publishing Co., 1969). Chapters dealing with major current protest movements and actions in the areas of civil rights, education, peace, and religion.
Cantril, Hadley, *Human Dimension: Experiences in Policy Research* (New Brunswick, N.J.: Rutgers University Press, 1967). Contributions of social psychological research to democratic processes.
Chafee, Zechariah, Jr., *Free Speech in the United States* (Cambridge, Mass.: Harvard University Press, 1941). The lucid thoughts of a great legal mind on this crucial subject.
Chafee, Zechariah, Jr., *Government and Mass Communications* (Chicago: University of Chicago Press, 1947, 2 vols.). A report prepared for the Luce Commission on Freedom of the Press.
Fortas, Abe, *Concerning Dissent and Civil Disobedience* (New York: Signet, 1968). A summary of the thoughts and experiences of a distinguished legal counselor and advocate for the rights of dissenters.
Free, Lloyd A., and Hadley Cantril, *Political Beliefs of Americans: A Study of Public Opinion* (New York: Simon & Schuster, 1968). A survey and consideration of the results of opinion studies.
Gulley, Halbert E., *Discussion, Conference, and Group Process* (New York: Holt, Rinehart & Winston, 1968). A text on discussion and conference methods.
Haiman, Franklyn S., *Freedom of Speech: Issues and Cases* (New York: Random House, 1965).

Key, V. O., Jr., *Public Opinion and American Democracy* (New York: Alfred A. Knopf, 1961). Roles of what is called "public opinion" in United States politics and government.

Luttbeg, Norman R., ed., *Public Opinion and Public Policy: Models of Political Linkage* (Homewood, Ill.: Dorsey Press, 1968). Broad consideration of the relations of propaganda, pressure groups, public opinion, political parties and leaders, and government agencies.

Mecklin, John M., *Story of American Dissent* (1934; Port Washington, N.Y.: Kennikat Press, 1970). Social historical treatise on dissenting movements in United States life.

Nevins, Allan, ed., *American Press Opinion: Washington to Coolidge* (Port Washington, N.Y.: Kennikat Press, 1969, 2 vols., re-issue). Running selection of outstanding press statements, chiefly editorials, on national and international affairs.

O'Neil, Robert M., *Free Speech: Responsible Communication Under Law* (Indianapolis: Bobbs-Merrill, 1966).

Sattler, William, and N. Edd Miller, *Discussion and Conference* (Englewood Cliffs, N.J.: Prentice-Hall, 1968). A text on available techniques.

Public Affairs Committee has published more than 400 pamphlets on a wide variety of subjects currently being discussed in the mass media. Their pamphlets combine a presentation of opposing views with a summary of objective evidence bearing upon each topic. A list of current pamphlets is available from the Committee at 381 Park Avenue South, New York, N.Y. 10016.